YOU CAN'T TRY
A DEAD MAN

You Can't Try a Dead Man is a poignant and inspiring true story that will leave you questioning true justice. I started working on Jeff Howard's case when in law school and have now been practicing law for over 13 years. Jeff's case still inspires me to find justice for every single client who comes my way.

—Jan Olson, Attorney at Law

Judee Howard has written a must-read primer for anyone interested in entering the criminal justice profession. *You Can't Try a Dead Man* teaches us the premise that our American justice system, although the best in the world, is not perfect. I am grateful to have been involved with Jeff's case as a law student and for many years since. My life and profession have been guided by witnessing Jeff and Judee's true story, their faith, and the love of Christ. Experience it for yourself.

—Matthew L. Olson, Attorney at Law/Chief Judge of the Crow Creek Sioux Tribe

I have worked in the legal field for over 25 years and became involved in Jeff's case in 2012. I truly believe this is a case where an innocent man was convicted and sent to prison. Occasionally our court system fails. In this case, we strive to correct that failure and allow Jeff to live the rest of his life a free man. Judee Howard not only tells a compelling and true story, but she also captures the equally important personal aspect that we cannot afford to forget.

—Kara Duncan, Paralegal

Judee Howard is a friend and a woman of integrity. She loves Jesus with all her heart and lives out daily what she believes. This is her story that deserves to be told. It's a story of injustice and long suffering. It's a story of faith in the midst of dire circumstances. It's a testimony that God is good no matter what. Judee and her husband Jeff are evidence that God's love knows no boundaries. And the love between a man and a woman knows no limits. Their story will touch your heart and inspire your faith.

—Linda Outka, Leadership Coach, Speaker, Trainer, Founder of Breakthrough Solutions, Inc. Author of *Pebbles in My Shoe: Three Steps to Breaking through Interpersonal Conflict*

I highly recommend this book on many levels. First, many on the outside have no idea how complex our court and corrections system can be. Judee and Jeff's story illustrates this complexity. On another level, since I have known this couple for many years, their story illustrates the redemptive power of faith in helping one to cope with broken situations. Jeff and Judee help us to see the ability of Christ to wring good out of any situation.

—Rev. Dennis Thum, Dean of the Chapel at University of Sioux Falls, Sioux Falls SD, Former Chaplain/Religious Activities Coordinator at the South Dakota State Penitentiary

YOU CAN'T TRY A DEAD MAN

The Untold Story of Injustice

JUDEE HOWARD

Some names have been changed to protect the privacy of individuals.

Printed in the United States of America
Published by Author Academy Elite
P.O. Box 43, Powell, OH 43035

www.AuthorAcademyElite.com

Paperback ISBN 978-1-64085-323-2

Hardback ISBN 978-1-64085-324-9

Ebook ISBN 978-1-64085-325-6

Library of Congress Control Number: 2018906192

DEDICATION

To Jeff, one of the most remarkable people I know. I am grateful and blessed to have entered your story, and you, mine. God knew we would be amazing together!

CONTENTS

FOREWARD

"Every time we witness an injustice and do not act, we train our character to be passive in its presence and thereby lose all ability to defend ourselves and those we love."—*Julian Assange*

The lucky chance that brought Judee Howard into my life more than a decade ago was invaluable. It was the beginning of a deeply rooted passion, a lesson on perseverance and a story that would touch my soul.

Judee and I had similar passions, we had social work degrees, and we had someone we love sitting behind bars. What we did not have in common is that Judee's husband, Jeff Howard, was incarcerated for a crime he did not commit.

Soon after my previous husband was incarcerated, I decided to go to law school to better support my children. I loved being a social worker and utilizing my skills, but the pay wasn't enough to take care of two little boys. From the first day of law school, I knew I wanted to be a public defender. I dreamed of defending someone's liberty and trusted that our system worked properly. That all changed when I met Judee Howard.

When I learned of Jeff's story, I grew curious and determined to review it to see if there was anything that could be done to help him. By this time, I was in law school and thought maybe I could offer something. Judee was determined to prove his innocence. I remember thinking, "Prove his innocence? I thought it was innocent until proven guilty?" It did not take long after receiving the boxes full of documents that the realization set in: an innocent man was sitting in prison. How could this be? This was unacceptable, so a few classmates and I started our journey to right this wrong never thinking that this process would last more than a decade. As Jeff Howard continued to sit in prison for a crime he did not commit, our journey continued. I witness Judee's undying faith in Jeff and their marriage, her perseverance in telling his story and the passion of the faith they share in God.

This road may be long, but it is one that must be traveled. For it is the duty of all of us to cherish freedom, fight against injustice and live with the harsh reality that at times, the freedom of an innocent man is stolen away by our justice system. Sitting idle is a dangerous place to be knowing a man's life has been stolen away from him. We all need to pave the road of good intentions with bricks of action, not only for the Jeff Howards of the world but for all of us that are at risk of finding ourselves in his shoes.

This book takes the reader on a journey through the life of an amazing man, a dedicated wife and the faith that keeps them going.

—Cheri Scharffenberg, Public Defender

PREFACE

On March 6, 1981, many lives were changed, not just Jeff's. Most significantly, a family lost a beloved son, brother, nephew, and cousin. They began a journey of grief, compounded by the fact that he had been murdered, many cannot fathom. It is an enormous tragedy. Jeff's heart, and mine, go out to them.

A NOTE TO THE READER

Sometimes we are invited into a story that seems too incredible to be true. That's what happened to me in the fall of 1993.

It started with my curiosity. When someone I had known earlier in my life was sentenced to prison (in another state). I wanted to know more about what prison life was like. In the early spring, I met a group of people with loved ones in prison.

Can you imagine having your son, husband, father, or friend known to the world only for the worst things he had ever done in his life? The love and commitment shown by this group of people had a profound effect on my heart and mind.

I once sat with a family during their son's and brother's trial. He had done unspeakable things to another human being. During a break in the proceedings, his mother whispered, "This is not the Ricky we know." She painted a picture of her son as a child, full of wonder, hopes, and dreams. Before the drugs and alcohol overtook his life, his future was full of possibilities. This heart-broken mother earnestly wanted me to know more about her son than what was in the court records, which would now define his future and how most others viewed him.

Twelve years later, I remembered that conversation when I worked with a non-medical in-home care agency. I met an older gentleman who had a physically debilitating disease. He needed me to know that he had been a successful businessman, a husband and father; not always this fragile shell of his former self. Inside his failing body, he was still sharp, engaging, and had lots to give the world, if we would listen and look past his physical frailties.

Too often, we judge a person by a tiny slice of their life. We think we know someone by what is happening at that particular moment when our lives intersect. People are always much, much more, if we will take the time to pay attention and open our hearts.

Little did I know when I was introduced to that precious group of people with loved ones in prison, that God was gently inviting me into a story that had been unfolding for more than a decade.

This story was, at first, hard to wrap my head around, and frankly, hard to believe. I am confident God invited me into the story but left the final decision up to me.

I spent many hours questioning: Would I have the courage to engage fully? Would I have the strength to endure, to love unconditionally, no matter what happened? Could I persevere over time without bitterness, loss of hope, loss of my faith?

As time went by I could see how the path of my life had uniquely prepared me to say "yes." That's when I fully entered the story of Jeff Howard.

CHAPTER 1

OPENING MY HEART

Hearing the stories of people whose loved ones were incarcerated opened my eyes, and heart, to a whole new world. Some of the stories were incredible, and most were heart-breaking. I wondered how people could bear such pain.

My only experience with the criminal justice system up to this time was "cop" shows. The shows rarely showed families of the "bad guys" in a favorable light. Reality is much more complex. I suddenly saw prison systems from a human perspective, and my heart fell in love with the families who endure so much.

As I developed new friendships in the group, I learned a lot of things I'd never even thought of up to this point. I asked one of my new friends if I could go with her to visit her husband and ask questions about what it was like to be in prison.

As I sat in the visiting room, hearing a husband and wife talk about their day, the kids, and their activities, I was struck by how ordinary it felt. I let my eyes wander and noticed many of the men looked like they could be my brother, father, uncle, or son as they visited with their families and loved ones.

There were tears shed at "hello" and "goodbye." These were human beings, known to most of the world by their terrible deeds. The families experienced immense pain due to their loved one's actions. What I saw that night was genuine love between parents and children; between husbands and wives.

I still witness this, although after many years, and wisdom that comes with time, I also see a lot of pain, betrayal, and broken hearts. I see healthy relationships and not-so-healthy ones.

That first visit to the prison forever changed me. I felt God leading me. He took the pain from my own life and brought me to see another perspective. But, God had more.

CHAPTER 2

JEFF + JUDEE

Through my involvement with the families of people in prison, I met Jeff Howard.

One of my new friends, married to a man in prison, asked me to write to her husband's friend. Jeff was, according to her husband, different than most of the men inside—whatever that meant. At first, I resisted. I did not want a relationship and I knew that was what he was looking for. There was enough on my plate. I needed to finish raising my three sons, and I had recently enrolled in college. I was also enjoying my new role as a liaison between prison officials and families.

After a couple of months, my friend asked me to read Jeff's letter. And, maybe, agree to write to him. He wrote an open letter, explaining a bit about himself and included a picture. I can't tell you what the letter said. It was the picture that convinced me it would be okay to write to him.

Jeff was sitting on a Harley, had on a muscle shirt, short shorts, a red bandana on his head, and visible tattoos. He also looked like a bodybuilder. Jeff Howard was most definitely not my type! I agreed to write to him until he found someone willing to be in a relationship with him.

It would be some months before I learned he was not a biker and the picture was from a fundraising event the Lifers' Group held for a local non-profit. The rest was real, just not the biker image I had of him. I love that about God—He met me right where I was and waited for me to be ready.

Jeff and I met face-to-face shortly after our first letter exchange. The group I was involved with was putting on a carnival in the underground visitation room. It was an event designed to strengthen family bonds between children and their fathers, or grandfathers, on the inside, by creating fun memories.

At the last minute, prison officials decided it was not appropriate for anyone on an inmate visit list to attend as a helper. That was our whole group, except for me! I had been to one such carnival at another facility, but I had never even been to this building, and I only had a small role in the previous event.

So, with two prison staff members and ten inmates, some of whom had also helped at a previous carnival, I entered the underground visit room with more than a little trepidation. I had heard Jeff would be helping, but to be honest, it was so busy and overwhelming, that it was all I could do to make sure things happened as I'd been instructed they should.

It was a fantastic evening, watching the unabashed joy of the children having fun with their fathers and grandfathers. At the end of the night, Jeff introduced himself.

It turned out, he had been by my side most of the evening and making sure that whatever I needed to have done, was done. I had observed the respect others had for him. I also noticed that he enjoyed himself, even though he didn't have any family of his own at the event.

He asked if I'd visit him and, after talking to the warden, I agreed to a "special visit." Inmates are allowed a certain number of "special" visits per year for people who are not on their regular visit list.

We ended up having several "special" visits, where I learned that he was a new Christian. I also learned the reason he was in prison.

—⟋⟍—

I grew up in a family where we were taught to be polite and not to hurt others' feelings. When Jeff said he was in for the murder of his roommate—and that he was innocent—I reacted on the outside more graciously than I actually felt.

The reason for his incarceration didn't surprise me—I knew he was in for life and that usually meant murder. But, I'd heard the familiar notion that "everyone in prison" says they are innocent.

I was a little disappointed in him but resisted rolling my eyes. To his face, I smiled and said something original like "Oh, okay." Undaunted, he proceeded to tell me his version of what had happened.

To be perfectly candid, what I was initially trying to do was to get him to come clean and admit his guilt. I just didn't believe stories like this happened, at least not to 99.999% of people. (I had seen the occasional news story about a wrongly convicted person).

I asked a lot of questions. I tried to understand his story, but I couldn't make sense of it. Part of that is because many years had passed, and part was because Jeff doesn't tell stories in a straight line. And, to be fair, I later realized he wasn't even around for most of the events surrounding his case. A lot of Jeff's information came from the trial. He didn't have actual memories of the events of the murder and investigation.

Ultimately, I agreed to be on his regular visit list and we began studying the Bible together. I went into it believing that if he was going to grow in his faith, he was going to have to set things right about what had happened and the reason for his life sentence. At least, that's what I thought at the time.

—⁂—

There is a genuine quality to Jeff, and at times, when I didn't know if I trusted him, that was confusing. I didn't know if he was conning me, if he really believed what he was saying, or if he was telling the truth. Jeff asked if I'd like to read his case sometime.

Growing up and into my early adulthood, I'd often been told I'd make a good lawyer. I loved to argue my point and was usually convinced I was right.

This observation hadn't been a compliment, but I'd heard it often enough to consider going to law school after I earned my undergraduate degree. I thought it would be fun and exciting to look at a real case and dissect it, so I agreed.

Jeff and I continued with our visits, drawing closer and letting each other into details of our lives. One day, I realized I was falling for Jeff.

No, no, no! This was not supposed to happen! I was happy being single and had absolutely no desire to marry again. I wrestled with God for several weeks begging Him to take this feeling away.

When that didn't happen, I let go of my fears and pre-conceived ideas about what my life should look like and peace filled my heart. I shared my feelings with Jeff and found out he felt the same way—he'd been respecting my wishes about our friendship and had mostly kept quiet about his feelings.

A few months later, Jeff asked me to marry him and we were engaged.

But soon, doubt started creeping into my mind. The reality of being married to a person with a life-without-parole sentence set in. Marrying Jeff might mean never walking hand in hand in the outdoors, sharing significant moments together such as our kids getting married, the birth of grandchildren, sickness, death, etc.

I told Jeff I couldn't marry him, but we could remain friends. For a few years, all I could focus on was what we could *not* have.

We continued visiting and established a pattern of reading the Bible and praying together. Not in a legalistic way, but with a desire to connect spiritually and share our faith. There's something special about praying together and hearing what's in each other's hearts that drew us even closer. How important all of this would become, we had no idea.

CHAPTER 3

JEFF, 1981

It was late morning when Jeff woke disoriented by the sounds of activity in the home. He had crashed on the living room couch at his friend Scott's house in the early morning hours after partying all night.

Lying there, Jeff remembered that this was the day he was leaving South Dakota to start a new life in Georgia where his friend Bob lived. He sat up and lit a cigarette to clear his mind and began planning what he needed to do before leaving town.

Pete, who also lived at the house, joined him. During their conversation, Jeff looked over to the end table and noticed a picture of the electric chair in the South Dakota State Prison. He turned the photo over and read the words written on the back out loud "They can only put you in there once."

He and Pete exchanged a few more words and then Jeff began preparing for his trip. Jeff had borrowed his roommate's backpack and was traveling light with just a few pieces of clothing, a sleeping bag, a blanket, pocketknife, lighter, bottle for water, and cigarettes.

A few hours later, he was dropped off at the interstate on the edge of town and began hitchhiking his way to Georgia.

It was March 6th, 1981.

Jeff had no idea that within a few hours a nation-wide manhunt for him would begin. His face and detailed description, including his tattoos, would pass around through media outlets and law enforcement offices across the nation. Police were on the lookout for him in South Dakota, Iowa, Texas, and Georgia.

Meanwhile, Jeff nonchalantly made his way across the country thinking about the opportunity to join his friend Bob. Traveling without access to television and newspapers, he was blissfully unaware of the horrific accusations—and how his future was now in jeopardy.

CHAPTER 4

LEADING UP

About two and a half months earlier, Jeff had met his roommate through a mutual acquaintance.

Jeff had recently completed his fourth stint in treatment for his drug and alcohol use. He was living in a halfway house and needed to find a place to live after his thirty days were up. Jeff had a job at a health food store and was well-liked by his boss. He was pretty sure she knew he used drugs but, as long as he did his work and showed up, she didn't say anything.

His roommate, who was eighteen years old, had recently moved back to Sioux Falls, and was working for his uncle. He was looking for a roommate to share his efficiency apartment and help with rent. He was introduced to Jeff who was also looking for an apartment.

When they met, Jeff was twenty-seven, well into his alcoholism and hard drugs, and mostly a loner. It was a convenient set up for them, but they didn't become close friends.

A couple of months passed and, even though he'd recently completed a treatment program, Jeff could tell the drugs and alcohol still had control over his life.

He applied for yet another treatment program, this time through the VA. There was an opening for him when he was ready. He had also kept in touch with Bob, a friend he'd made during his last stay in treatment. Bob had moved to Georgia to get a new start, and they had talked about Jeff coming to stay with him. There he would have an opportunity to work and attend school to learn a trade.

Jeff was a hard worker when he wasn't drinking and knew he could do anything he set his mind to.

He hadn't yet decided whether to go for more treatment or join his friend Bob but knew he needed to do something soon. So, in preparation, on the night of March 2nd, Jeff borrowed his roommate's car, took $20 from his wallet, and drove to his hometown to pick up some personal items.

His roommate was sleeping when he left so Jeff left a note to let him know what he'd done and where his car was since he might not be back in time for him to go to work.

Jeff had borrowed the car before, and he was aware that his roommate could get a ride to work with his uncle if needed. It was a ninety-minute drive to the small town of Mt. Vernon, South Dakota. Jeff had some things he wanted that were at his dad's place, and he intended to be back the next morning. Instead, while parked outside waiting for his dad to wake up, Jeff was picked up by a deputy sheriff for an outstanding warrant. It would be a couple of days before he returned with the car.

—⁓—

After a court hearing Monday morning, March 5th, Jeff used a pay phone to call his boss to let her know what had happened and that he was heading back to Sioux Falls. She told him he was fired and informed him his roommate was upset and had reported the car stolen.

When Jeff arrived back in Sioux Falls, he stopped at his friend Scott's house. Scott lived with his sister Janice, and her boyfriend Pete, with whom Jeff was also acquainted. He arranged to meet up with Scott later after he returned the car.

Jeff drove around a bit, looking for his roommate. He hoped to avoid arrest for stealing the car and give the car back to its owner before the police found him. Eventually, they met up at a mutual acquaintance's house.

According to Jeff and early police reports from witnesses, the two had some heated words, but then things calmed down. Jeff agreed to move out immediately since he had been planning to leave town anyway.

They went back to the shared apartment, and Jeff packed some of his belongings. He asked if he could use his roommate's backpack, for more comfortable travel, in exchange for the remainder of his portion of rent he had already paid for that month. Jeff filled a duffle bag with the rest of his belongings and left them at the apartment to be sent to him later.

His roommate drove him to Scott's house, and they said goodbye. Jeff heard Scott was up the street, so he left his backpack at the back door and walked over to meet up with him.

No longer having a place to live, and needing an immediate option, Jeff decided to head to Georgia to live with Bob. That night, he called the number he had for friends of Bob's to let him know he would be heading to Georgia the following day. The next few hours were spent watching a ball game and partying with Scott and friends well into the early morning hours. Midday on March 6th, he headed to Georgia, as planned.

—⚒—

Early, the morning of March 6th, his roommate's uncle went to the apartment to pick up his nephew for work. He found the door ajar and his nephew's body lying on the sofa with a trickle of blood on his forehead. Someone had murdered him during the wee hours of the morning.

CHAPTER 5

PHYSICAL EVIDENCE

The police began their investigation in the small, first-floor, efficiency apartment where Jeff and his roommate had been living, and where the body had been discovered.

It appeared the victim had been struck with a single blow to the head by a small blunt object. He was lying face up, blanket pulled upward, where it appeared he had been sleeping when someone murdered him. According to reports, this was what the police found:

- The kitchen window was open—police surmised this was where the intruder entered the apartment.
- A screen that matched the window was found in the adjacent parking lot, not far from the window.
- The front door was ajar when the victim's uncle arrived, likely where the intruder exited.

- A spoon with white residue and a knife were lying on the kitchen counter, indicating someone had possibly shot up with drugs the previous night. A syringe cover was lying on the kitchen floor.
- Jeff's packed duffle bag was lying on the floor and taken into evidence.
- An empty billfold was on the floor next to the body.
- A hammer was found hanging from the molding in the kitchen. It was taken into evidence since it appeared to match the size and shape of the head wound on the victim.
- The victim's car was missing and found the next day a few blocks away.

Other evidence collected later and used at the trial:

- The backpack, found with Jeff at the time of his arrest, was taken into evidence.
- On July 1st, a few days before the trial, Pete turned a key over to the police, saying it was a key to the victim's apartment, given to him by Jeff.

More than a decade later, when I sat down to become acquainted with the case, I fully expected the evidence to point toward Jeff's guilt. But I ended up with many questions, instead.

The police fingerprinted around the kitchen window and in the immediate area inside. They found no fingerprints—as if it had been wiped clean. I puzzled over this part of the investigation: Why would Jeff feel the need to wipe off fingerprints when he had lived there up until only a few hours earlier?

The window screen, tossed across the parking lot, was not examined for fingerprints. An officer testified at the trial that the window screen had not been tested, reasoning that since the window sill didn't take fingerprints, the screen wouldn't have, either. However, reports show that an officer's fingerprint was left on the window sill at the time it was dusted for fingerprints, indicating it *could* take prints but had been wiped clean. So, if someone had purposely wiped fingerprints off the sill and nearby kitchen counter before leaving, they may have still left prints on the screen tossed across the parking lot. But, since it was not tested, a piece of evidence may have been missed.

There were no other fingerprints taken at the scene. Not off the front door or knob, the room where the body was found, nor other areas of the kitchen, including kitchen faucets. The spoon and knife found on the kitchen counter were not tested and the syringe on the kitchen floor was not tested nor taken into evidence.

The police surmised the intruder had entered through the kitchen window. It was later established that Jeff left an apartment key with someone when he left town. I wondered why Jeff would have needed to enter through a window if he still had the key to the apartment?

No hair and fiber samples were collected from anywhere in the apartment. There was no recording of the police checking for footprints or other evidence from around the perimeter of the crime scene with the exception of the screen from the kitchen window. A few days later footprints were used to identify an intruder trying to break into the apartment. Had there been footprints or other evidence that were missed outside the apartment during the initial investigation?

There was no testing on the billfold. It was "handled carefully" by the officer who found it, but it was not taken into evidence.

The hammer hanging on the molding in the kitchen was sent to a lab for testing. The lab reported that synthetic plant fibers and animal hair were found on the claw of the hammer. There was no blood or human substance found on the hammer, and only smudges were found when tested for fingerprints. The lab report supported Jeff's story that his roommate had come across the hammer in the trash a few days earlier and hung it on the molding in the kitchen. Still, this hammer was repeatedly referred to as the murder weapon at trial.

The victim's car was located the next day, parked two blocks from where Jeff had spent the night at his friend Scott's house. I noted that it was also where Pete lived. The car appeared to have been in the process of being vandalized. The police found one neighbor home at the time of discovery who said he'd noticed it parked there the previous afternoon.

The police did not collect fingerprints, hair, or fiber samples from the car, and it was released to the victim's family shortly afterward. There is no mention in the reports that the police went back to question other neighbors after the initial finding to see if anyone else had seen anything.

The deceased's family was allowed into the apartment on March 9th to retrieve some of the victim's belongings. On March 11th, the family received the remainder of his belongings from the apartment, and the residence was turned back over to the landlord.

When Pete turned a key over to police on July 1st, almost four months later, he said Jeff gave him the apartment key before he left town so that he could take Jeff's roommate's stereo. He told police he hadn't turned it over sooner, "Because either he neglected to or perhaps because he had planned to take the stuff Jeff Howard had told him he could have." The police were unable to verify the key was the actual key to the apartment since the landlord had changed the locks months ago. At trial, Pete testified that he did not keep the key to burglarize the house but that he kept the key in order not to incriminate Jeff. I found this statement ludicrous. Besides the fact that Pete changed his story from only a week ago, every prior statement he made to the police incriminated Jeff.

Jeff admitted that he gave the apartment key to his friend Scott on March 6th, before leaving town, so that he could steal his roommate's stereo. But, if Jeff had just murdered his roommate, why would he give someone a key to the apartment where they could find the body?

As I dug into Jeff's case, I questioned how the police built a case strong enough to convict him. Things didn't add up. I began to question my original assumptions. What if Jeff was telling the truth?

CHAPTER 6

WITNESSES

The police learned of the argument that had taken place between Jeff and his roommate and interviewed those who had been present. The opinions included in the police reports indicated that while the argument was initially heated, it had calmed down and Jeff agreed to move out that night. Witnesses said he and the victim left amicably to go back to the apartment so Jeff could pack up his belongings.

The police took statements from the people who had partied with Jeff the night before. The party had moved to various locations throughout the evening, and into the morning. They needed to establish a timeline for the events leading up to the murder.

—⁓—

On March 7th, several people voluntarily came to the police station together with Pete to give their statements.

Pete told police he read about the murder in the newspaper that morning. He said Jeff had stayed at his house the night before having left town.

Pete claimed he'd seen Jeff that night at a party and they had been together briefly, but then Pete left the party early and went home. The next morning, he found Jeff asleep on his couch.

Pete said in the morning they'd had a conversation where Jeff admitted he might have killed the kid he'd been living with. He said Jeff had noticed Pete's picture of the electric chair and picked it up and stated: "They can only put you in there once." He failed to mention, until the trial, that those words were already handwritten on the back of the picture.

Pete's girlfriend, Janice, corroborated his story about Pete coming home early the night of March 5ᵗʰ and to overhearing the conversation where Jeff admitted to killing his roommate. Pete also told police he had checked his kitchen drawer after reading the account in the newspaper and found his hammer was missing. There was nothing in the newspaper article that indicated the murder weapon might be a hammer or the size and details of the injury. I wondered why there wasn't more information about Pete's missing hammer. Why wouldn't the police look into that more? This seemed like a critical component, especially in light of the forensics report that would later come back on the hammer found in Jeff's and his roommate's apartment.

—⁂—

After the case made the news, a local couple called the police station to report who they felt was responsible for the murder. They named four people. The police dismissed this as unreliable information. Yet, on March 9th, one person who was named in the report broke into the apartment. After the police received the call about someone breaking in, they located the suspect in the neighborhood and identified him by the footprints found in four places around the outside of the apartment. The suspect's story about how he learned of the murder changed during the interview process, and one officer felt he knew more than he was telling. The reason he gave for being at the apartment was that a couple of weeks earlier, the victim told him if something ever happened to him, he could have his "stash of narcotics and his stereo." No further follow up was done with this young man. Years later, when I began my investigation, I tried to follow up with him. I wondered if he might have known something that could be helpful, but he had recently passed away.

CHAPTER 7

JEFF'S ARREST

After the police learned about Jeff and the victim's argument and that Jeff had left town, Jeff seemed like a likely suspect. They soon learned of Jeff's plans to head to Georgia and found out where his friend Bob lived. Jeff hadn't kept where he was going a secret.

Detectives widened the search in case Jeff changed his plans, but the Georgia Bureau of Investigation still had officers visit people who lived in the trailer court where Bob lived, leaving a description of Jeff and a warning to call them if he showed up.

Jeff arrived dirty and tired at Bob's on Thursday, March 12th. Bob told him the police had been there looking for him because they thought Jeff might have "hurt someone" back in Sioux Falls.

Jeff didn't know why the police would be looking for him and thought it was a mistake. He told Bob he was tired and wanted to take a shower and would talk to the police after he cleaned up. Jeff didn't seem at all concerned about Bob's news.

While Jeff was in the shower, Bob's home was surrounded by law enforcement with their guns drawn, ordering them both out of the trailer. Bob let Jeff know the police were there and left the trailer. Jeff hurriedly finished his shower and dressed before walking out with his hands in the air.

The police had Bob on the ground with a gun to his head when Jeff stepped out. They didn't speak as Jeff was handcuffed and driven away. Bob wouldn't know what happened to Jeff until years later.

Jeff waived extradition and was brought back to Sioux Falls the next day, Friday, March 13th. That's when he learned what had happened to his roommate and began to see the gravity of the situation.

—∞—

Jeff had never been more confused or scared in his life, and he had no one to turn to for help or support.

He didn't know who was saying he had murdered his roommate. Why were they saying he did it? And he wondered why anyone would want to murder him. Nothing made sense.

He was locked up in the county jail, and the only people he could talk to were other inmates in his cell block. It felt a little better to have people to talk to, but they couldn't help him, and they couldn't alleviate the fear that was taking over his mind and heart.

Jeff was no stranger to jail or prison. He had been in and out of the state training school for juvenile delinquents as a teenager and had been arrested and jailed due to his alcoholism several times. He had also been to prison twice for minor offenses.

But, this was different, and he knew it. He felt powerless and utterly alone.

CHAPTER 8

JEFF'S SIDE OF THE STORY

After the arrest and learning about the charges against him, Jeff remained in jail until his trial. He could hardly comprehend that his roommate had been killed, let alone fathom why he was the one blamed for his murder. He had to rely on his court-appointed attorney to make the case that he did not kill his roommate.

Because of his lifestyle, Jeff had burned bridges with his family and didn't have contact with them. He assumed they knew of his arrest and the charges since it was all over the news. He hoped they would contact him, but they didn't.

In today's world, two attorneys, experienced in criminal law, would be appointed to handle the defense in a murder case. In 1981, things were very different.

Having no resources to hire a lawyer, Jeff was appointed an attorney by the court in the week following his arrest. He became nervous about his attorney when other inmates reported that his lawyer had little, if any, experience in criminal law. They told him that his attorney typically handled personal injury claims.

Jeff remembers meeting with his attorney a few times to discuss his case. Jeff gave him the names of people who could be character witnesses for him as well as Scott and Bob's information to verify his story of what happened. He had confidence his friends would corroborate his story and verify he could never do such a thing.

Jeff learned of the state's evidence through news stories on television and in the newspaper. Occasionally he'd get more anecdotal information from other jail inmates coming through the system.

News travels fast in criminal networks, and Jeff's case was big news. In 1981, murder was an even more uncommon occurrence in South Dakota than it is today.

Jeff's account of what happened the morning of the murder, and up to leaving town later that day, didn't match Pete's account.

—⋙—

Jeff recalled waking up on the couch and having a conversation with Pete. He thought it was odd that there was a picture of the South Dakota electric chair on the table and so he picked it up and read the words handwritten on the back.

The conversation with Pete was brief, and he may have shared his plans to leave town. He remembered people coming and going to work, including Scott coming back from work after noon. He recalled the presence of Pete's girlfriend, Janice, and her young daughter.

Jeff's focus that morning was on getting a ride to pick up his food stamps and then to the interstate to begin hitchhiking to Georgia. Pete mentioned he needed to pick up food stamps also and borrowed his friend Wayne's pickup and gave Jeff a ride. Jeff later learned that Pete did not pick up food stamps that day.

Before leaving town, Jeff gave his apartment key to Scott, telling him he could go over and steal his roommate's stereo. Years later, when finally interviewed, Scott corroborated Jeff's story. They had not spoken since before Jeff left town, March 6, 1981.

Early in the afternoon, Wayne dropped Jeff off south of town by the Interstate. Jeff needed cash, so Wayne gave Jeff a few dollars in exchange for some of his food stamps.

Jeff spent the next six days on the road, hitchhiking to Georgia.

—⁓—

As Jeff awaited trial, he read the newspaper accounts and wondered why Pete would set him up. He had no idea how they could build a case against him when he didn't do it. He didn't understand why the newspapers were reporting so negatively about him.

Deep down, Jeff believed that when he told his side of the story, he would be free to go. He just had to wait until his day in court.

The days passed slowly.

CHAPTER 9

STATE'S KEY WITNESS

As the trial date neared, Pete surprised everyone by claiming amnesia. Two weeks before the trial, responding to a subpoena, Pete claimed he did not know Jeff Howard or anything about the case. Pete was the prosecution's key witness. This was a case primarily built on circumstantial evidence, and Pete's testimony was the key to convicting Jeff.

On June 30th, a week before the trial, the State's Attorney asked the judge if Pete's earlier police statements could be used at the trial in lieu of Pete himself since he was still claiming amnesia.

Pete had given a signed statement to police detectives, about two days after the murder occurred, that said Jeff had admitted committing the murder. Newspaper reports state that prosecutors told the judge they "virtually have no case" if the signed statement of Pete was not permitted as evidence in the case.

At the pre-trial hearing on June 30th, the judge asked if Pete was an important witness. The transcript reads the State's Attorney having said "...without [Pete] the State, I would have in my own mind, I don't think we have much of a case. I'm not going to say that I don't expect to get to the jury, but I will say that we would have a very difficult time obtaining a conviction without [Pete's] testimony. I cannot tell you what I would do, whether I would dismiss or whatever..."

The judge ordered tests to verify the amnesia. It was then that Pete admitted he was lying and did not have amnesia. According to a news report, Pete said he lied about the amnesia because he felt his cooperation with the State had fostered threats on his life.

Pete said someone had come up from behind him in an alley in his hometown, Sioux City, Iowa, and hit him. The next thing he knew he woke up in the hospital. He said he was afraid because he did not know who had done it, implying that it might have to do with testifying in Jeff's case.

Many years later, files from the State Attorney's Office were turned over to Jeff. They included medical reports from the incident in Sioux City that had happened in April 1981 and told a very different story from Pete's account.

According to the reports, it was not an attack from behind, but a face to face fist fight. One report states that Pete was apparently struck in the left jaw by another person. He then fell back and struck the back of his head on concrete and was unconscious for two to three minutes. Another report reads, "Friends state patient was hit in mouth with fist and then fell and hit head on concrete..." A Neurology Consultation Report says Pete told them he was involved in a fist fight and stated that he got struck on the face and fell over, striking the back of his skull.

The same medical reports gave Pete a secondary diagnosis: "He is consistent with sociopathic behavior." A South Dakota detective, investigating Pete's claim of amnesia, traveled to Sioux City and spoke with local detectives. In a police report, the South Dakota detective writes "[Pete] has been cooperative only when he is in a bind, and the cops have the goods on him...one trait of [Pete]'s is that he likes to brag about his exploits to his friends." The same report states that the South Dakota detective contacted a sheriff about charges Pete had pending in Iowa. During the trial, the detective testified that Iowa offered to give Pete a benefit by dropping the charges in Iowa if it would help the case against Jeff.

On July 20, 1981, after the trial was over, Jeff's attorney received an envelope from an anonymous source. It contained a Pre-sentence Investigation Report from a 1978 1st Degree Robbery conviction for Pete. The report quotes Pete stating that he [Pete] had been psychologically evaluated and the results of the evaluation "in the opinion of the psychiatrist he is a sociopathic individual with an explosive and violent temper." Pete also stated in the report that he felt he had "good control of himself" at that time.

During the trial, Pete testified that he had not had "the experience of cooperating with law enforcement officials to get a lesser sentence or recommendation." But, in the previously mentioned Pre-sentence Investigation Report, it states, "If granted probation, he would finish work that he is doing for the Iowa law enforcement officials, and he would then attempt to get relocated."

On the last page of the report, a Sheriff is referenced saying, "The defendant has been cooperative and helpful to his department. He further stated that he feels the defendant has been honest in his dealings with the Sheriff's Department." The report is not dated, however, at the top of this page Jeff's case number is handwritten.

—⟊⟊—

At the time of Jeff's trial, Pete had charges pending in Sibley, Iowa for 3rd-degree burglary. An officer in Iowa indicated that the rest of the time to be served on this charge could be used as a "lever" for Pete's testimony in Jeff's trial if needed. The police captain in South Dakota denied on the stand that this "leverage" was ever used, but Pete served no more time in Iowa.

—⟊⟊—

Pete's trial testimony also conflicts with his statements made to the police shortly after the murder and the week before the trial.

He lied to the police about the length of his hospitalizations when he had his head injury in Sioux City, indicating more time spent in the hospital. In police reports, he stated he had been in the hospital in Sioux City, Iowa for two weeks and then an additional week in Sioux Falls, South Dakota. In actuality, he spent about five days total between the two hospital stays.

Jeff's attorney was not made aware of Pete's medical reports and so could not use the information in them to bear on the credibility of Pete as a witness.

Pete's statements to the police on July 1st about Jeff handing him a key, conflict with his testimony on the stand only a week later. During the trial, Pete testified that he asked Jeff "...What about your stuff?...I asked if he wanted me to go over and get them...and he said,

'All I really have over there is my stereo.' He pulled a key off a key ring and handed it to me."

As mentioned earlier, his story about the picture of the electric chair changed. In the police report the day following the murder, Pete implied Jeff's comment "you can only sit here once" was made about having killed his roommate. On the stand, Pete admitted the words had been previously inscribed on the back of the picture.

During the trial, Pete said he had only met Jeff about three weeks before the murder and indicated they hardly knew each other. Jeff says that he met Pete when they did time in the penitentiary together in 1978. They didn't know each other well, but they did know who each other was. In the weeks leading up to the murder, Jeff sold some drugs to friends for Pete. They were well acquainted even if not friends.

CHAPTER 10

THE TRIAL

The day of the trial finally arrived. It had initially been scheduled for June 1st, a week shy of three months after the murder. The state's attorney had asked for an extension, and the trial was rescheduled for July 6th with the judge's caution that he would not delay the trial again.

Jeff arrived in court clean shaven and with a fresh haircut. He had been given street clothing to wear at the trial. He wore the same outfit all week.

Every day, when walking into the courtroom, Jeff's eyes scanned the room to see if anyone had come on his behalf. And each day he found himself alone, with only his attorney for support. He knew he had burned many bridges, but it was still a bitter reality that he was alone in this battle when the odds seemed so stacked against him. He longed for the support of his family—anyone who would care what happened to him.

He was concerned and apprehensive, but down deep believed that when he told his side of the story, the truth, he would be released and this would all be over.

Monday, July 6th, was devoted to selecting a jury. Potential jurors were advised this was a circumstantial case and asked if they would give "fair credence" to the testimony of a felon (Pete) with three former convictions.

By the end of the day, five women and seven men were selected, along with two alternates. The trial would begin the following day and was expected to be complete by the end of the week.

Over the course of the next two days, Jeff sat incredulous as witnesses were called to testify against him, putting words in his mouth he knew he had never said. Fear took over his heart and mind. He could only sit in silence as he listened to the lies and case built on circumstantial evidence.

Being locked away while awaiting trial put Jeff in a type of a bubble. He didn't have people on the outside, advocating and following up on leads for him. He depended on the expertise of his attorney; and the assumed non-biased and impartial state's attorney's office which has the financial and staffing resources to investigate crimes. Jeff's attorney could have requested funding to do his own investigating, but it doesn't appear he did. Jeff had to trust everyone will do their utmost to investigate thoroughly and discover the truth about what happened. But while locked away, he had no control over this process.

Years later, when I questioned a senior partner at a firm about the experience of Jeff's habeas attorney's capability in the courtroom, I was told: "You people want a Perry Mason, with everything wrapped up in a neat bow." Well, yes, that's what any of us would want.

As Americans we expect everything to come out right and just in the end.

Jeff learned at the time of the trial that his attorney did not intend to call the witnesses he had requested to help with his defense. The two key witnesses who could corroborate his story were Scott (who he'd spent the night and early morning hours partying with), and Bob, present at the time of his arrest. Scott had moved to Colorado to avoid being subpoenaed to testify.

Many years later, when questioned, Scott shared that he had left town because Pete was pressuring him to back up his story and he knew it was a lie. He didn't want to go against Pete and Janice. (Janice is his sister, and she was testifying on Pete's behalf.) Jeff's attorney decided not to subpoena Bob and did not call any character witnesses.

When Jeff learned his attorney had not called any witnesses on his behalf, he realized it would be his word alone, against everyone else's.

On Thursday Jeff took the stand. His story contradicted the state's witnesses, yet he still hoped the jury would see through the lies and believe him.

Remember, this was a case built on circumstantial evidence, and the state didn't feel they had a case without Pete. Being a free man, Pete had time to gather people together. Some had even changed their stories from their original police reports. Jeff's attorney did not point out the discrepancies.

The witnesses who said in police reports that Jeff and the victim's heated words had cooled down before they left, now stated, under oath, that Jeff had said he wanted to kill his roommate.

The Coroner stated that time of death was between 1:30 a.m. to 5:00 a.m. with the bulk of evidence pointing to between 3:00 a.m. to 3:30 a.m. According to testimony in police reports and during the trial, a witness stated she drove Scott and Jeff back to Scott's house around 3:30 a.m. She knew this because when she arrived back home, she set her alarm clock for work and noticed the time was 3:45 a.m.

Jeff testified that after they arrived back at Scott's, they cooked some pheasant and ate it before Scott headed to his room and Jeff sacked out on the couch. Without Scott's testimony to back this up, Jeff's accounting of time for the evening did not carry as much weight. Scott was also not there to back up Jeff's word on having given the apartment key to Scott before he left town.

There was other evidence not received, or at least not followed up on, which could have impeached some of the testimony of the state's witnesses.

One of those witnesses was Janice, Pete's wife. Pete and Janice were living together at the time of the murder but married a few weeks later. Janice backed up Pete's story, that he arrived home earlier the evening preceding the murder and that she had overheard a conversation between Jeff and Pete where Jeff asked if South Dakota had the death penalty and asked about the electric chair. She said Pete then got out a picture of the electric chair and showed it to him.

In fact, on July 1st, the same day Pete turned over a key to the police, Janice had been subjected to a polygraph test and had shown deception on questions about Jeff implicating himself in the death of his roommate. Either Jeff's attorney hadn't known about the polygraph test or outright failed to raise questions about her testimony based on the results. It is likely he had not known about the polygraph since the examiner's report is dated July 10th, the last day of the trial when the jury was already deliberating.

Wayne, the person who had dropped Jeff off at the interstate and whom Jeff had said had given him cash for some of his food stamps, lied and said he hadn't purchased food stamps from Jeff. Police reports state that Wayne's girlfriend had brought in a book of food stamps the police verified as having been issued to Jeff. The information doesn't seem like a significant point, except that it's another time where Jeff was made to look like a liar.

Wayne had been on parole and had violated the terms of his parole, due to hanging around with people he was not supposed to. Trial testimony states Wayne was granted immunity from the revocation of his parole in return for his testimony against Jeff.

The final day of the trial wrapped up with Jeff's testimony, the lone refuter of evidence against him, and closing arguments.

In closing arguments, the State's Attorney blatantly told untruths or mislead the jury:

- He repeatedly held the hammer found at the scene in the air and called it the murder weapon, even though forensic evidence would indicate otherwise.
- He stated the murderer, "Had to shoot up at the scene," referring to the spoon and knife on the counter, and further stated that, "The only person connected in this entire case who shoots up is Jeff Howard." In fact, there is no record of any testing for needle marks or drug use for anyone else connected with the case, except the victim.
- He also stated several times that the victim slept in front of his door during the few days Jeff was gone with his car because he was afraid of Jeff. Recorded testimony of witnesses state very

clearly that the victim slept in front of the door because he was afraid he would not wake up when Jeff came back. Testimony also said that the victim was a very sound sleeper. Witnesses were misquoted to make his point.

One of the inferences made against Jeff was that he left town on March 6th, leading the police to suspect him because he had "fled town."

First, Jeff had been planning to leave town, either for treatment or to go to Georgia, even though that date had been moved up due to his roommate asking him to leave immediately. He told people he was leaving and made calls in their presence to Bob in Georgia.

Second, on March 6th Jeff remained in Sioux Falls into the early afternoon. He appeared to be in no hurry to leave. Jeff was acutely aware of the arrangement between his roommate and his uncle to pick him up in the early morning for work if he didn't show up.

Third, why give the apartment key to someone if he had murdered his roommate, knowing they would discover the body?

Furthermore, Jeff had six days on the road to check to see if he was wanted and could have changed his plans, but he didn't. When informed the police were looking for him, he could have turned and fled.

None of Jeff's actions spoke of a person fleeing the scene of a crime.

Jeff's attorney was no match for the impassioned young state's attorney, making a name for himself in his first murder case. The jury was dismissed and told to return the next day for deliberations. The judge asked them to be prepared to go into the weekend if necessary.

CHAPTER 11

VERDICT AND SENTENCING

On Friday, July 10th, the jury deliberated only four hours before making their decision.

During the trial, Jeff's attorney asked Jeff if he could speak to the judge about asking for a plea deal. Jeff didn't see why he should plead out for a chance at a lesser sentence when he was innocent. He told his attorney no.

Nothing can prepare a person to receive the words Jeff would hear that day. During the entire trial, he'd never given up hope that when the jury heard his side, they would believe him because he was telling the truth.

Hearing the word "guilty" nearly caused his legs to buckle out from under him. The shock was almost unbearable. Jeff could barely breathe. Fear and disbelief consumed him. His legs didn't want to move. He could hardly take it in. A thousand thoughts went through his mind, including "what ifs" and "why me?" He felt like his life was over.

The emotions were so overwhelming at that moment that even feeling anger was impossible. Jeff remembers only feeling numb and cold.

Jeff knew what his sentence would be. South Dakota only had two options for a first-degree murder conviction, and an agreement to take the death penalty off the table had already taken place.

The only sentence left was mandatory "life without the possibility of parole." He would be locked up until he died.

Ultimately, a life sentence is a death sentence without a date and determined method. Jeff was twenty-seven years old with much of his life still ahead of him.

He doesn't remember the trip back to his jail cell. Formal sentencing happened on August 3rd. The day came and went. Jeff was relocated from jail to prison.

The prison wasn't unfamiliar territory. Jeff knew what awaited him. After all, he'd been there before but never thought of it as his home. Now, a concrete-block six by nine-foot bathroom with a bed and desk would be his home—for the rest of his days.

CHAPTER 12

JUDEE'S BACKGROUND

Before 1993, I had never been to a prison or known anyone who had been to prison. I had no frame of reference for understanding issues surrounding corrections, the judicial system, impact on families, etc. It was as foreign to me as the planet Mars.

My life started out very different from Jeff's. A lot had to happen for me to be willing to meet Jeff and enter his story.

I grew up in a suburb of Los Angeles. My parents are still married to each other, and they raised us in a Christian home. Our faith wasn't just something we did on Sundays; it was how we lived our lives every day. I didn't think we lived a sheltered life, but there were definitely many things I had never been exposed to.

We lived on what I would say is the lower end of middle class. My father worked hard in his job as a mechanic for the school district and took side jobs to help make ends meet. I am the oldest of five. We are close in age which kept my mother busy. She began working from home as a music teacher when I was seven and started attending college when I was in my teens.

I was somewhat rebellious as a teen. My rebellion was mostly toward my mom, and I didn't get involved with drugs or alcohol. While I was a handful and contrary with my parents, I was also active in my church youth group. The "Jesus Movement" was getting started and had a positive impact on my life.

I met Michael at youth group when I was seventeen. He seemed as passionate about his faith as I was. Against counsel, we married when I was eighteen, and he was nineteen. We were young, but we loved Jesus, and we loved each other. That was all we needed, or so I thought.

Life was idyllic for a few months. Then things started going haywire. My loving husband began to show erratic and strange behaviors. I'm sure my stubborn streak didn't help, but I don't believe it was the primary cause of our problems.

Never before had I imagined that a husband would hit his wife. We separated and reunited a few times in our short five-year marriage. During that time I gave birth to two sons.

It would be 15 years before Michael was diagnosed with a severe mental illness. Even though many years had passed since our marriage had ended, it was a relief, because now the behaviors made sense. I also felt great sadness—for the beautiful soul I'd known for such a brief time; but mostly for our boys, who would never know that man.

Shortly after my first marriage ended, I re-married, ignoring advice to let time pass. Apparently, I wasn't done being stubborn. I felt my boys needed a father.

After all, I didn't have any first-hand knowledge of anyone who had raised children alone.

My second marriage didn't fare well either. Though Jim had a kind heart, he said he was not ready to be married and left before our sixth anniversary. We had one son, so now I was raising three boys on my own.

Divorce was almost unheard of in our family, and here I was, divorced twice. I carried a lot of shame. In the following years, I made some poor choices and, sadly, my boys suffered for those.

My spiritual life withered at times. I felt God must be disappointed in me, but I knew he loved me and would never leave me. I just didn't know how to recover the closeness I felt we once had. Going to church didn't even do it for me, although I continued to attend because I wanted the boys to know about Jesus. There are lots of good memories mingled with the hard times.

My primary support as a single parent had been a close friend, who turned out to have ulterior motives and hurt our family deeply. My guilt and shame prevented me from sharing with anyone what we had experienced.

One night after the kids went to bed, I fell to my knees on the living room floor. I was broken and crying out to God in earnest. I was tired of carrying this burden alone. I distinctly remember saying, "Please God, do whatever you need to do and make me totally dependent on you."

It was the spring of 1990. I had no idea what God would do with this prayer, or if He would do anything at all. But it was an earnest cry from my heart, and it stayed in the forefront in my mind for years to come.

It began slowly. First, it was a desire to move away from Southern California. I knew that had to be from God because I was reluctant to pursue new experiences.

In the early summer of 1991, my brother and his family moved to a small town, south of Sioux Falls, South Dakota.

I'm not sure he meant to invite me, but he gave an open invitation for anyone to join him. He sent pictures of South Dakota in June. All I saw were wide open spaces, green grass everywhere, and blue skies. Blue skies are rare in the Los Angeles Basin.

Shortly before this, I had received an annual bonus from my boss and a hefty tax return. I felt like it was a now-or-never opportunity. I just knew God was calling me to South Dakota.

Anyone who knows me knows that geography and I are not friends. I had no idea where South Dakota was on the map or what it would look like to live in the upper Midwest.

People kept cautioning me that it was, "Really, really cold up there." If you've only lived in Southern California your whole life, there is no frame of reference for temperatures below zero and wind chills in the minus twenties and even colder.

But, I knew this was God's leading—otherwise, I would never have set out for lands unknown. It was totally out of my character and comfort zone.

To say the boys were not excited would be an understatement, at least for two of them. They were two years apart in school, and the oldest was entering high school. We were moving to a town of 800, just south of Sioux Falls, where K-12 was under one roof. At least my middle son thought it was an adventure.

Adjusting to our new life was much harder than I thought. Culture shock being just one issue—South Dakota and Southern California are like two different countries, compounded by moving to a small town. And then there's winter...

The first year, I cried often, wondering what I had done to my family, but there was no way to turn back. We muddled through, and things got much harder. It would be a few years before things improved for us. A lot of changes were happening in our little family. A couple of years after arriving in South Dakota, we were on the cusp of homelessness. We moved to the larger town of Sioux Falls to be near more resources.

We ended up on public assistance, which was incredibly painful, but also into a housing assistance program that encouraged secondary education. We continued to struggle, but now we had some safety nets to prevent us from being on the streets, and I was hopeful for positive changes.

Sometimes I wondered if I'd misread God's communication with me. So much of what was happening seemed out of my control, and yet I had to depend on God more and more. But, did the answer to my earnest prayer that night in 1990, on the living room floor, need to be this hard?

CHAPTER 13

JEFF'S BACKGROUND

Jeff grew up in a small prairie town in South Dakota. He is the oldest of six with five younger sisters.

When Jeff was a young boy, they lived on a farm. He enjoyed everything about the farm—helping his dad fix the hog barn, getting chicken eggs with his mom. He enjoyed the freedom to run around and play with nobody watching. He remembers walking a quarter-mile to another farm to play with a friend.

When he was five or six, his family moved to town permanently. Jeff didn't want to go. He buried his teddy bear in a box of corn cobs in the barn, hoping he would be back to get it.

Eventually, he adjusted to living in town and made friends. He enjoyed the freedom to play kick the can under the street lights after dark and riding his bike all over. In a community of around four hundred in the 1960's, just about everyone knew everyone.

The local school housed kindergarten through 12th grade and classes were small. There were usually three to four cousins in his class. He struggled in school and was held back in 5th grade, putting him in the same class with his twin sisters who were just eleven months younger.

Jeff enjoyed nature and could often be found playing outdoors, either alone or with cousins and friends from school. He enjoyed playing make-believe in the cornfields and shelterbelts, a line of trees planted to protect areas surrounding a farm from the wind.

When Jeff was seven or eight, things began to change between him and his father. His father seemed angry with him, and instead of letting him play with friends, Jeff was often expected to do hard chores such as chopping wood and mowing. Jeff saw his father as a taskmaster who was tough to please, and no matter how hard he felt he tried, his father was not happy with how he did his work. In Jeff's opinion, the work seemed excessive in comparison to his sisters and his friends.

There were good times too, such as when their family took trips to visit relatives. His dad let him play and be a kid when they were with other families. He spent a couple of weeks with his grandpa and a couple of weeks with his uncle and enjoyed those times without fear. But at home, things were different.

Jeff admits he wasn't the most compliant child but didn't feel he deserved the anger and frustration unleashed on him. When it was time for his father to arrive home after work or being out, Jeff would begin to feel fearful. He would often hide out in the fields or shelterbelt until he knew where things stood that day. Jeff never knew what mood his father would be in, and it didn't seem to be dependent on what he did or didn't do.

As he grew older, he tried hiding the bruises on his body when he had to shower after gym class. Other kids in town made fun of him and he learned to make up stories as to what happened. People knew what was really happening, but in those days, no one knew what to do and figured it was a family matter. He didn't know why his father seemed angry at him, but since he wasn't that way toward his sisters, he figured he must have done something to deserve it.

On Saturday mornings, Jeff would walk to his great-grandma's house. She had one of the first color televisions in their small town. He would eat breakfast and watch cartoons in the morning. He felt safe there and didn't mind helping with work in her yard such as picking apples and potato bugs, mowing the lawn, and pulling weeds. It felt like she appreciated his hard work. Sometimes his sisters came with him.

The fear of his father affected many areas of his life as he grew up, including problems with authority that would plague him for years to come.

At the age of nine, Jeff had his first sip of alcohol and would continue to seek it out when he found it easily accessible. As he neared his teens, he learned that alcohol created a buffer against the emotional pain he was feeling. He would sneak alcohol from friends, family, and even the supply of Mogen David wine stored in the church basement for communion.

The fear in his heart turned into behaviors that became hard to manage. He often snuck out at night and started hanging out with bigger kids who got into trouble. When he was fifteen or sixteen, an ex-con taught him how to burglarize businesses.

He stole alcohol and other things just for the thrill of it. One time, Jeff was with two younger friends and an adult bought them some booze. They were pulled over by the police, and their parents were called. His friends' parents came and picked them up, but no one came to pick up Jeff. Finally, an officer took him home, and he received one of the harshest beatings he ever had.

Some nights, he could overhear his parents discussing what they should do with him. He wondered about his future as well. He didn't have any more answers than they did.

While most of his interactions with his father were hard, there were good times too. Occasionally, his father took him along to work on projects, and they talked and worked well alongside each other. His father taught him how to work hard and have a good work ethic.

Jeff enjoyed playing basketball and football. As a young teen, he unleashed his pent-up anger on the football field. He had worked up a high tolerance for pain and didn't mind tackling or being tackled hard. The coach liked him, and it became one of his favorite pastimes.

But his drinking and behaviors caught up with him. He and a couple of friends caused considerable damage on school property, and while no charges were filed, Jeff was responsible for paying for repairs. As a freshman in high school and just fifteen years old, he found himself expelled from school for good.

His Uncle Ernie hired him to work on his farm, so Jeff could earn money to pay for the damages and put some money away into savings. It turned out to be a good year for Jeff. He felt safe and enjoyed the hard work. Since he was only fifteen, the money he put into a savings account required his dad as a co-signer.

It took about a year to pay for the damages he owed. Instead of continuing with this positive direction, when the debt was paid in full, Jeff left his uncle's farm and moved to a nearby town. There, he found other runaways like him. He moved around a lot and often slept on someone's couch.

At age sixteen, Jeff forged his dad's signature at the bank and withdrew most of the money he'd saved. He used the money to buy pot and headed out with friends to the "Days of '76," a cowboy and rodeo event, in Deadwood, South Dakota. After that they went on to Denver, drinking and getting high. On their way back to South Dakota they were caught with the remaining pot. His dad came to get him and bring him back home. He stayed for a couple of weeks and then ran away again.

Jeff worked spot jobs around town, but often his drinking got in the way, and he'd be asked to move on.

At the age of seventeen, he got into trouble again and was put in the state training school not far from his hometown. His mother came to see him every week, bringing him cigarettes and making sure he had what he needed. He earned his GED while there.

After his release at the age of eighteen, the training school set him up to work for an older couple in a nearby town, but Jeff ran off and got into more trouble. This time, his grandma and an aunt stepped in, and he moved to Pierre, South Dakota, a few hours away from his usual stomping grounds. But it wasn't long before they had a falling out and he was asked to leave. He was then hired to work on another nearby farm. Once again, he enjoyed farm work and being outside.

On June 11, 1972, another of Jeff's Aunts showed up at his work to bring him the news that his mother had died. She had a sudden heart attack while napping on that Sunday afternoon. She was only 38 years old.

Jeff was eighteen years old, and his mother's death devastated him. His aunt drove him home, and he walked through the house, looking for her, not believing she was gone. At that time, he believed his mother was the only person who truly loved him. Her death left a hole he didn't know how to fill. His father still had five daughters to finish raising.

A few weeks after his mother's death, Jeff was in a tractor accident. The tractor overturned and ran over him, nearly killing him. After some time in the hospital, the doctors told him not to work throughout the summer while he healed from his head injury. His father allowed him to move back home while he recuperated. Being back home, he missed his mother even more and felt incredibly alone.

—∞—

After a couple of weeks at his father's, some friends he'd met from the training school stopped by to see if he wanted to move to Sioux Falls with them. He went with them but was soon back into drinking and doing stupid things, so decided to join the Marines to get away and start over.

Jeff enjoyed and excelled at the rigorous physical requirements of boot camp. Without drugs and alcohol, he felt better than he had in a long time. He pushed himself physically and could outrun almost everyone else.

If only he could have maintained this new lifestyle, things might have turned out very differently for Jeff.

When he went home on leave after boot camp, Jeff got right back into his bad habits and hanging out with old friends. He was late getting back to the base by a couple of days, but they let him back in. However, his pattern of drinking continued whenever he had the chance to leave the base.

One night, in May of 1973, he was out drinking with a friend who didn't return when he said he would. Jeff got impatient and since he had the keys to his friend's car, decided to go back to the base alone. Unfortunately, being too drunk to drive, Jeff wrecked the car before he arrived at the base.

He was arrested and convicted of "Misdemeanor Temporary Larceny" and received a sentence of one day to two years in the North Carolina prison system. He was also discharged from the Marines.

The prison camp in North Carolina was hard labor, and after a few months, he and a buddy hatched a plan to escape. It worked, at least for a while, and Jeff hung out in a nearby town, continuing in his old habits. After a few months, he made someone mad and decided it was time to leave. Since no one from the prison had come looking for him, he decided to move back to South Dakota and meet up with old friends.

Amongst the familiar, he went back to his old ways of drinking, getting high, and moving around a lot. Nine months after he had walked away from prison, a sheriff showed up at his door and sent him back to North Carolina. The escape added another misdemeanor to his record and 90 days to his sentence.

He was placed at another prison camp. Just a couple of weeks after returning from his first escape, the opportunity and temptation to escape presented suddenly and he impulsively decided to try it again. He was only gone a few hours this time before authorities caught up with him.

This escape earned him his first felony and doing time in a more secure facility. It also added 120 additional days to his sentence. His one day to two-year sentence took two and a half years to complete.

The environment in this North Carolina prison was much different than anything he'd experienced before. He was a skinny white kid from South Dakota where fair-skinned people were in the minority. For the first time, he was sought out by predators.

Paralyzing fear returned to him. Inmates in this prison dealt with conflict using prison-made shanks and stabbings were not uncommon. Jeff didn't like hurting people, so he tried to stay to himself, but he lived in constant fear that he would be next. He became prejudiced, something that would take years to unlearn.

Eventually, some long-timers befriended him and helped him serve out the rest of his time safely. It was during this time that someone introduced Jeff to hard drugs and the use of needles to get high.

He was released in September 1975 and returned to South Dakota.

After he had escaped the first time, Jeff had met a girl. They wrote to each other while he was in North Carolina. While he was gone, she had gotten pregnant and had a baby girl. After his release, they hooked up, and in February 1976 they were married. They had a baby boy in the fall of that year.

Jeff tried to settle down. He enjoyed being a father to his son and step-daughter. They brought a lot of joy into his life. But the drinking and drug use continued, spiraling out of control. As Jeff felt less in control of himself, he tried controlling others around him. His marriage was in trouble, but he couldn't stop using or controlling. His behavior only worsened.

In November 1977, while drunk, Jeff stole fifty dollars' worth of hotdogs from a school cafeteria. He received a two-year sentence for 3rd Degree Burglary and was remanded to the South Dakota State Penitentiary.

In April 1978, a judge suspended his sentence, and he was a free man. But, a year later, he violated the terms of his release and was sent back to complete his sentence. He was released again in July 1979, early, due to good behavior. By this time, his marriage was over. Over the next couple of years, Jeff drifted in and out of treatment programs in Iowa and South Dakota and moved around a lot. Two of those times were involuntary commitments due to getting in trouble while drinking. He carried deep-seated anger toward anyone in authority and viewed his misfortunes as things that happened "to" him. He could find no purpose other than his next high and numbing the pain in his soul that never seemed to leave him. He felt worthless and unlovable. Jeff sometimes let women get close to him, but most of the time he held people at an emotional distance.

Occasionally Jeff would cross paths with someone who wanted to help him, but most of the time his interactions were with people like himself—lost and drifting; using alcohol and drugs also to manage their pain. He continued his downward spiral.

Jeff trusted few people if any, and any money he made went to support his own habit. His drug and alcohol lifestyle taught him that being a loner was a way to stay under the radar. It also made him a perfect candidate to set up for the murder of his roommate.

CHAPTER 14

PRISON LIFE

The world Jeff was would soon enter is a place many of us are unlikely to experience.

Prison is a noisy place with constant clanging doors, the occasional beep of metal detectors, incessant chatter and yelling between inmates, loudspeaker announcements, and toilets flushing. TVs and radios require headphones, but that doesn't stop vocal reactions to intense tv shows and competitive sports.

Each day is the same. Days center around the routine of hurried meals, doors locked, doors unlocked, count times, inspections, showers, cleaning, and occasional program opportunities.

If you're lucky, you can look forward to mail, phone calls, and regular visits. Sadly, that is not the case for everyone.

Prison life becomes a predictable routine and a community all its own. If you're lucky enough to have a job, your days have at least some purpose. Fixing toilets, doing laundry, working in the kitchen, or cleaning common areas provides some relief and a sense of purpose. Some jobs teach a trade or offer meaningful work for a non-profit organization.

Sometimes you are fortunate enough to make friends. But, friends can be transferred to another section or prison facility at any time. Outside of face-to-face contact, direct prisoner to prisoner communication is rarely allowed. It may be years before you connect again, if ever.

Prisons are made up of people from every type of background and walk of life. Many prisoners come from a background of poverty.[1] Mental illness is common, and inmates are sometimes highly medicated or acting out behaviors that can cause havoc and be hard to manage. Every type of deviant behavior is present inside the walls.

It is also a place filled with remorse as many committed crimes that they can hardly believe they did, either in the heat of passion or under the influence of drugs or alcohol.

These feelings and issues, left unresolved, lead to behaviors that require a new set of rules for survival— survival physically, mentally, and emotionally. It is an environment where the weak are often preyed upon.

For many people, time and memories stop when they entered prison. They relive those memories over and over, in the attempt to not forget their life on the outside. They often tell stories from those days over and over, as if they just happened.

---

[1]   Rabuy, Bernadette and Kopf, Daniel. "Prisons of Poverty: Uncovering the pre-incarceration incomes of the imprisoned." Prison Policy Initiative. https://www.prisonpolicy.org/reports/income.html (accessed May 23, 2018).

I've seen families struggle as institutionalism sets in, making it difficult for those locked up to relate to loved ones on the outside. With a reduced world-view, there is a tendency to become less concerned with the needs of others. And, when your world becomes so small, things bother you that, living on the outside, a person would hardly consider.

Family connections are lost or weakened as life on the outside moves on, and the inmate's world can become self-focused. Inmates worry about what is happening with their loved ones but have no control over anything and cannot offer any help. Sometimes loved ones even pass away without the opportunity to say goodbye.

As you might imagine, depression and suicidal thoughts are not uncommon.

—∿—

I've heard it said that you don't need to punish people after they go to prison; prison is punishment enough. Loss of freedom is enormous.

CHAPTER 15

SOUTH DAKOTA PRISONS

"The Hill" in Sioux Falls is an imposing structure. Constructed in 1881, it is on top of a hill on the north end of the city. It was built as a territory prison before South Dakota became a state in 1889. It's had some updates, but it remains an old building. The outside is constructed of South Dakota block granite and could be considered beautiful from a distance, even with the bars on the windows and barbed wire fencing around the perimeter.

Inside, The Hill, resembles an old-style penitentiary, one you might see in the movies. Walls are painted with drab colors and windows are small, dingy, and sometimes in disrepair. Each hall of cells is five tiers high and between ten to twenty cells long. Cells house between one and three inmates. Preference for single cells usually goes to long-time lifers. Besides a limited number of personal items, cells contain a bunk bed, a small desk with shelves, a toilet, sink, and a plastic chair. They measure approximately six feet by nine feet. Cells are constructed with three walls of cement block, coated with numerous layers of paint, cement floors, and barred doors that shut with a loud clang. Doors are locked by staff members whenever an inmate has no reason to be outside their cell. South Dakota still has the death penalty, with the death chamber located on The Hill next to Health Services.

Life is full of schedules and rules. Most rules are for safety reasons. On The Hill, cell halls and the dining area are not equipped with air conditioning. In the summer, tension runs high as everyone swelters—staff and inmates alike.

Winter weather conditions are extreme in South Dakota, so outside recreation is limited to just a few months of the year. The rest of the time inmates are either working, attending a program such as a religious service or class, earning a GED, eating, or in their cells—with few exceptions. Recreation is held inside, in a crowded gymnasium.

Many changes have taken places over the thirty-seven years since Jeff entered prison. In 1981, the entire South Dakota prison system housed close to 700 prisoners.[2] In those early years, inmates were known by name to the warden and most of the staff.

As of April 30, 2018, there were almost 4,000 persons housed in the South Dakota adult prison system,[3]

---

[2]   U.S. Department of Justice: Bureau of Justice Statistics. "Prisoners in 1982." *Bureau of Justice Statistics Bulletin,* April 1983. https://www.bjs.gov/content/pub/pdf/p82.pdf

[3]   South Dakota Department of Corrections. "April 30, 2018 Adult Corrections." *Adult Corrections, Adult Population, April 30, 2018.* https://doc.sd.gov/documents/AdultPopulationApril2018.pdf

which now includes several more structures spread out over the state.

On The Hill, visitation takes place in a room in the basement level of the prison, beneath the kitchen and dining area. From the entrance lobby, you walk down a flight of stairs and a tunnel corridor, pass through a metal detector, and two metal doors that make a racket when opening and closing. There have been attempts to update this room, such as painting over the wood paneling, but it is anything but homey.

Most of the South Dakota prison facilities allow contact visits. Visitors and inmates are allowed a brief hug at the beginning and end of their visit and may hold hands during their time together. There is a dress code, enforced with officers' discretion.

A section is set aside for those times when there is no contact allowed. Inmates and their families and friends visit with glass between them and talk by phone.

Visits are closely monitored by cameras, micro-phones, and officers nearby. Visitors and inmates alike try not to think about the intrusion. For security's sake, this is necessary, but that doesn't make it any easier.

In 1993, there was a need to expand the prison to house the growing prison population. Two high-security buildings surrounded by fencing and razor wire, and trustee building were added on the northeast side of The Hill, called the Jameson Annex. These facilities are more modern and have air conditioning. However, fam-ilies still experience the same scrutiny during visitation.

CHAPTER 16

THE EARLY YEARS FOR JEFF

Jeff began his life sentence in a familiar place - The Hill, the same place he spent time in 1977-1979. But, this was different because he knew he wouldn't be out anytime soon.

For a country boy who loved the outdoors and solitude, the thought of being locked up for the rest of his life seemed like an unbearable burden.

His anger against anyone in authority continued to fester inside. He was angry at the system and all those who lied at the trial. He was angry at all authority figures. But, he was also angry with himself. He wondered how he had come to this. Down deep, he knew he had made a mess of his life, even if he wasn't guilty of killing his roommate. But, he could see no way to find answers or change things, so instead of dealing with his feelings, he soon reverted to his old ways of numbing the pain.

In those days, it was easy to get away with making *hooch*, prison alcohol, sometimes also called *pruno*. You could also get drugs. Jeff spent his first years in a bit of a fog, working on getting high one way or the other.

His behavior earned him numerous write-ups and five stints in "the hole" for 30-40 days at a time. In the hole, you are confined 23 hours a day to your cell with little contact with anyone else. Its purpose is punishment with time to contemplate your actions. Unfortunately, it had very little if any, reformative impact. Jeff really didn't mind being in the hole because he liked the solitude. He spent his time reading books—mostly westerns.

Jeff's case had been highly publicized. It was no secret what he was in for and for how long. There was no use in telling anyone he was innocent. Most prisoners spend the first few years appealing their case and seeking a reduction in their sentence, whether innocent or guilty. Jeff's situation appeared no different.

Those early years were lonely. Jeff had two outside acquaintances who showed up a few times in those first months. In 1986, his sisters came to tell him his father had a brain aneurysm, and he was allowed a half-day with his father and sisters at the hospital. That visit marked the beginning of an effort to make peace with his father. His father survived, but, outside of this brief time spent with family, years went by with Jeff experiencing hardly any outside contact.

Jeff was a loner, but in time he made a few friends who enjoyed sports and lifting weights.

In 1984, Roger entered prison and he and Jeff became friends almost immediately. Over time, they grew to trust each other and became best friends. According to Jeff, they did a lot of stupid things together, but they could also be serious with one another and talk on a deeper level than Jeff allowed with anyone else on the inside. Roger wasn't a lifer, but he had a significant amount of time to do.

Both Jeff and Roger had a soft spot for the younger guys and felt it was their duty to keep them in line. They also felt protective toward those who were vulnerable to predators.

Jeff was bullied growing up and victimized while doing prison time in North Carolina. If Jeff has an intolerance, it is toward bullies. He didn't hurt anyone, but it became common knowledge that if you needed to stay safe, you should seek out Jeff and Roger.

Prison has its own set of rules and hierarchy. "lifers" are typically granted a particular respect, depending on their crime. Being a lifer, and in for murder, infers that you have nothing to lose. There is generally mutual respect amongst lifers. After all, this is their home. In those early days, they were given some latitude by staff to help keep things in order.

Despite his initial reluctance to mingle with others, Jeff eventually joined various clubs, such as the Weight Club, Jaycees, and Lifer's Group. These groups helped him build some unity with others. As they worked together to help each other grow they were also encouraging each other to do things that were constructive rather than destructive. Slowly, this began to have a positive impact on Jeff's mindset.

CHAPTER 17

POST-CONVICTION REMEDIES

From the time he entered prison in 1981, the procedures of post-trial remedies moved forward in Jeff's case. Jeff continued to believe things would be set right and trusted his attorneys. With no income, he was declared indigent and continued to have court-appointed attorneys assigned to his case.

In law, post-conviction refers to the legal process which takes place after a trial results in a conviction and the defendant is sentenced. Post-conviction relief takes place through legal actions, known as filing an appeal or a writ of habeas corpus. The case then progresses through various levels of government including the county where the crime and original trial occurred, the state level, and then the federal courts.

An appeal is used to correct errors that occurred during a trial. No new evidence is allowed to be introduced. If you think the trial judge made a legal error during the course of your criminal case, then you file an appeal.

A writ of habeas corpus (habeas) comes into play if you want the court to consider evidence the trial judge or jury might not have had at the time of the trial. To win a habeas petition, you have to prove that the legal error that occurred actually resulted in a loss of the defendant's rights.

Immediately following the trial in 1981, Jeff's attorney filed an appeal to the State Supreme Court. But, the original conviction was affirmed.

In 1982, a habeas was filed with the US District Court of South Dakota and in 1983 relief was denied.

In September 1983, Jeff learned that Pete, the state's key witness against him, had taken his own life. He died by hanging. There was never any mention of a suicide note. But, as Jeff would learn later, Pete may have had a motivation tied to the case, for taking his life.

Soon after Pete's death, Jeff heard through the prison grapevine that several people were willing to attest that Pete had told them he had committed the murder that sent Jeff to prison. Jeff had always wondered why Pete had helped build a case against him. To this day, one of our biggest frustrations is that we can only speculate about Pete's motive for murder. For all we know, that information died with Pete.

In December 1983, Jeff received an unexpected letter from Rick, the person whose house he and Scott had partied at before leaving for Georgia that fateful day. Rick had not been present the night or early morning hours of the party at his house, but he had seen Pete the following day and had information for Jeff.

Rick apologized for not coming forward earlier. He had, "Kept quiet for Janice's sake, and didn't want to be accused of snitching on Pete." In the letter, he said Pete had come over the morning after the murder and made Rick give his word he would never tell anyone what he was about to tell him. Pete admitted to, "Killing the boy and pinning it on Jeff." Rick said he felt sick over it but was close to Janice and couldn't "Rat Pete out" since she and Pete were married.

Rick shared that Pete told him he got the key to the apartment off Jeff when he was with him that night, "And killed that boy." Pete had told Rick he was scared but planned to pin it on Jeff since he knew Jeff and his roommate had argued the night before the murder, and that with Jeff leaving town it would help make him look guilty.

According to Rick, Pete asked him to come to the police station and back his story, but Rick had refused. He said he did talk to the police, but only told them he'd been out of town and so didn't know anything.

Rick also wrote that Pete was excited because he said he'd most likely get out of some other trouble he was in by pinning this on Jeff. In his letter, Rick offered to testify to all of this and hoped it wasn't too late.

In 1984 Jeff's case was assigned to the Public Defender's Office to file a writ of habeas corpus in the county in which he was convicted. He turned the information about Pete's confessions to the murder, over to his attorney, including the letter from Rick.

The case changed hands three times in that first year, but affidavits from the witnesses to Pete's statements were obtained. Five people were willing to testify as to what Pete had told them.

One other significant source was not adequately followed up on. Many years before the murder, Pete married a woman named Pam, and they had three children. Their marriage had ended in divorce and Pam had custody of the children, but they occasionally visited their father.

In 1984, Pam contacted Jeff's attorney to share information her then 12-year-old son, Jason, had told her. Shortly before Pete's death, the children had visited him. Jason claimed to have overheard his father say he killed someone with a blow to the head with a hammer and sent another man to prison for it.

The attorney arranged a meeting to get Jason's statement. There are notes in the file about an arranged meeting, but for some unknown reason, the meeting never took place.

The habeas case stayed with the public defender's office from August 1984 until April 1988. Jeff had several encouraging back-and-forth letters and a face-to-face meeting with his attorney. However, in March of 1988, Jeff suddenly received a letter stating she believed his habeas application was meritless and she was not going to pursue the matter.

Jeff was confused and devastated. He never learned why the attorney changed her mind, even though he inquired. He didn't have enough knowledge of the law to know that his rights were being violated. He certainly didn't know what to do next.

Years later, Jeff learned that her response was inappropriate. It was up to a court of law to make that determination—not his attorney. Since the habeas never made it to court, the affidavits including Pete's admission of guilt and notes about Jason's testimony would lie dormant in a file in the Public Defender's Office for several years.

Jeff, while discouraged, wasn't one to give up. On his own accord, he continued his quest for freedom. He wrote several attorneys, asking for help. However, he was turned down time after time. He had no money and no one to advocate for him on the outside. The case stood still until 1994.

CHAPTER 18

A NEW KIND OF FREEDOM

By 1986, Jeff had been taking stock of his life. In the process an internal transformation began. He never lost hope for his freedom, but he finally realized that if he was going to have any chance at that freedom and living a different life, he needed to make a real change in his thinking and attitude.

As he noticed others making the same mistakes over and over, he realized he was also looking at himself. As Jeff puts it, he became "sick and tired of being sick and tired" and felt like he had lost track of who he was supposed to be.

Jeff had lived much of his life being angry and getting high or drunk, and he was beginning to understand where it had gotten him. The life he was now living was not where, or how, he wanted to spend the rest of his days. He decided this was also not how he wanted to see himself or have others view him.

Jeff stopped smoking and using profanity. And, July 4, 1986 marked the beginning of his commitment to sobriety—and he has been clean and sober since. Jeff joined Alcoholics Anonymous (AA) and began to learn what it meant to take responsibility for his actions. He started the journey to let go of the fear and anger that had imprisoned him for so long.

Initially, a driving motivation to continue in this vein was that lifers were offered the opportunity for inside/outside trustee status. A chance to be outside the prison walls during the day was enticing and something he longed to experience.

In 1986, Jeff earned this privilege, and he had no intention of losing it due to stupid behaviors. With this status, he was able to go shopping for supplies for the prison and inmates. He also got to take part in the maintenance of a camp for children with disabilities. He reveled in the trust placed in him and had a renewed sense of purpose.

In March 1987, Jeff transferred to the prison facility in Springfield, South Dakota. Daily fresh air and more opportunity to spend time outdoors was a welcome change.

Being a co-ed facility made it all the better, although women lived in different dorms and contact was limited. Even when there was a mingling of the two genders, physical contact was not allowed. There was a one-foot rule, meaning there had to be a minimum of twelve inches between a man and a woman.

During this time, Jeff earned a degree in welding and held a job doing maintenance work. He was good with his hands and didn't mind getting dirty. He had always been able to figure out how to repair machinery, plumbing, and just about anything that needed fixing.

Being busy and using his natural abilities again made him feel useful and he took pride in his work.

He also worked hard to better himself by attending classes and groups that helped him change. As AA puts it, he had to change his "stinking thinking." He was a willing learner and excited to embrace a new way of looking at himself and the world around him.

Jeff earned the respect of staff and inmates alike. At one point, he married another inmate, opening his heart to love someone. The marriage didn't last long after she was released and went back to her old lifestyle. He took it hard but resisted turning back to his old ways. He sought counsel and worked through it.

In May of 1993, there was a terrible riot at the prison in Sioux Falls. People were injured, and some of the buildings were damaged. Prison officials, understandably, decided they needed to review and modify some of their practices.

Security tightened up considerably, and changes began happening that affected many of the long-timers who had earned trust over the years. The prison system implemented a new classification system that put limitations on how and where inmates were housed, resulting in much more restriction of movement.

Jeff had been in Springfield for six and a half years up to this point and had enjoyed a level of freedom where he sometimes went outside the walls with no restraints. He was trusted and respected, as were many others.

Through no fault of their own, lifers, now re-classified as violent offenders, had to be placed in a more secure setting. Those who had been in Springfield were brought back to Sioux Falls in June of 1993.

It was a tough time for the long-timers, especially those who had earned inside/outside trustee status. They had to re-adjust to life back on The Hill and a much more restrictive lifestyle. A lot of staff turnover took place, during this time, and with each new officer, trust had to be established.

If you want to better yourself in the prison system, there are opportunities, but you usually need to seek them out. In the early days, more schooling and programs were available to everyone, and you earned "good time," time off your sentence, by taking advantage of those opportunities.

Many inmates played the game of attending programs to look good before the parole board. But Jeff found himself diving into every opportunity whole-heartedly. He was on a mission to become a new man.

One of the most life-changing experiences for him was when "outsiders" came inside the walls, usually for religious programs. Those outsiders showered the inmates with kindness and love.

Jeff hadn't experienced this kind of love and acceptance in a long time. Here were people, taking time out of their usual routines, away from their families and busy lives, and investing in people the rest of the world seemed to have forgotten. It touched him deep in his spirit and inspired him to learn more about what made them give so selflessly.

Many inmates, including Jeff, rarely, if ever had visits from their own families. Yet here were people with no motive except caring for others, who showed up and spent time with them. Their sacrifice impacted Jeff and helped him open his heart to God's love. His heart began to soften, and he started to learn to not only receive love but eventually to give love, also.

CHAPTER 19

BELIEVING JEFF

Soon after meeting Jeff and trying to understand his story, Jeff asked me to look at his case. It took a while to gather the paperwork, but in the summer of 1994, I finally had enough to begin the process. I spent the entire break after my freshman year of college, reading through numerous police reports, motion hearing and trial transcripts, post-trial affidavits, forensic reports, attorney correspondence, etc. Whew!

When I had gone through everything, I had two questions. First, how did they convict Jeff with so little evidence? Second, what was I missing? It was clear that we were missing some of the paperwork and I wondered if finding it might provide answers.

I set about to read it through again and made notes this time. I began to consider that Jeff might be telling me the truth, although I doubted my layperson's ability to come to any definitive conclusion. I'd recently met

Jean, a third-year law student, and asked if she would take a look at Jeff's paperwork and let me know what she thought.

Amazingly, she saw what I saw. A circumstantial case, that when all the evidence was put together from both pre- and post-trial, seemed a convincing argument for a wrongful conviction. Or at the very least, cast reasonable doubt as to Jeff's guilt.

In the meantime, I also took my questions to Jeff. Often his answers were vague, or "I don't know." Finally, after showing my frustration, he said to me "I don't know because I wasn't there."

Oh! If what he told me and what I was reading was the truth, that made sense. Also, a few years had passed since he'd last read through his paperwork.

I had to admit, I was beginning to believe him, but there was part of me that held out. I also wondered why God would draw me into this story. Was it because I was going to be an attorney?

Besides just starting college and busy with my teenage sons, I had no experience and absolutely no idea how to help this man.

Early in this part of our journey, I was referred to a former judge to ask about recourse for an actual innocent man. I shared Jeff's story, and while empathetic to the situation, he told me that, at this point, thirteen years after his conviction, it didn't matter if Jeff was innocent or guilty, only if he had had a fair trial. So many years had passed and overturning his case was not a likely option.

I was stunned. It didn't matter if Jeff was innocent?! I was so new to all of it, and I could not wrap my mind around this. How could anyone leave an innocent person in prison? There had to be a solution. Having a stubborn streak can sometimes be a good thing.

In the meantime, Jean realized that since Jeff's 1984 Writ of Habeas Corpus was still open and pending with the court, it could be picked back up and continued. Jeff filed the necessary paperwork, and a judge signed an order appointing Jeff new legal counsel for the filing of the habeas. Still an indigent, he was assigned a court-appointed attorney.

Martin was an experienced attorney, however not in criminal defense work. But, he would spend many hours on Jeff's case over the course of the next couple of years. We met regularly, and I appreciated his candidness and that he genuinely cared about representing Jeff to the best of his ability.

Martin obtained court orders for missing information and completed Jeff's file with the missing police reports and other paperwork on his case, including files from the State's Attorney's Office, some of which Jeff had never seen.

Martin also located Bob, Jeff's friend from Georgia, now living in another state, a family man with a good job. Bob was incredulous that Jeff was in prison. He had never heard what happened after Jeff's arrest in 1981. He couldn't believe Jeff had been found guilty of murder. Bob's story backed that of Jeff's that Jeff wasn't concerned when Bob confronted him with the news that he was wanted in South Dakota. Martin arranged a deposition from Bob.

As we tried to locate people who had written affidavits regarding Pete's admission of guilt to them, we discovered most had died.

Rick was still alive and affirmed his original letter to Jeff and affidavit.

In the State's Attorney's file were copies of receipts for relocation money paid to Pete by both the Police Department and the State's Attorney's Office. The receipts totaled $700. Also included were the medical reports regarding Pete's assault in Iowa before the trial. Jeff's previous attorneys had not had access to this information.

In the winter of 1994, Jason, Pete's son, was found, living in Sioux Falls at the time. He spoke to me first and then to the attorney, Martin. Jason's story was still the same after all these years. He'd overheard his father say he'd killed someone with a hammer and sent an innocent man to prison for it. Jason said he'd tried to make it right, but nothing came of it and that it had always bothered him.

For various reasons having to do with things going on in Jason's life, Jason and Martin did not meet to obtain an affidavit, and Jason took his own life in May of 1995.

As we drew close to the habeas hearing set for mid-June of 1996, I decided to do some more investigating on my own. I still wasn't 100% convinced of Jeff's innocence, and I needed to discover some more things for myself.

On June 11, 1996, a week before the hearing, I made a trip to Sioux City, Iowa. Sioux City is about 90 miles south of Sioux Falls. Almost everyone affiliated with Jeff's case, including Pete, was from Sioux City and had been connected to one another, mostly through drugs and crime at the time of the murder. Now, many were no longer part of that lifestyle but still connected in some way. Before Jeff had gone to prison, he was acquainted with some of them but had never really been part of Pete's Sioux City crowd.

I was accompanied by Mike, a young man from my church. He and his wife had recently moved to Sioux Falls. Mike was a a recent graduate of the School of Mines in the Black Hills of South Dakota and hadn't yet obtained employment. He asked if I'd like company when I shared my plans to go to Sioux City and mentioned that I was nervous about it.

Later, Mike told me his other motive for going. He had concerns about my story and felt, that as a scientist, he might see things I didn't.

Jeff's best friend in prison, Roger, had been released in 1994. He and Jeff remained in contact after his release and Roger wanted to help with the case in any way he could. He was also from Sioux City and knew a few people closely affiliated with those involved in Jeff's case.

Roger introduced me to Donna, to whom he had been married many years before. Donna just happened to be sister to Pam—the same Pam who used to be married to Pete and was Jason's mom. Donna was instrumental in setting up the meetings that took place that day.

We planned to meet with Pam, Pete's ex-wife and Jason's mom; Janice, Pete's girlfriend at the time of the murder and wife during the trial; and Scott whom Jeff had been with the night/morning of the murder.

Our first stop was Pam's house where her daughter, Stacey, also Jason's sister, happened to be visiting from out of state. It had been only a little over a year since Jason's death. Pam said she didn't know how she could help. She was uncertain Jason had heard right because the account Pete had told his family and friends, in 1981, about testifying in a murder case, was different from what Jason overheard his father say.

Since Sioux City is in a different state, news accounts from Sioux Falls, South Dakota, wouldn't have likely been broadcast there.

I shared what the police reports and an autopsy report said—that Jeff's roommate's death was due to a single blow to the head with a blunt object, probably the head of a hammer or similar type object.

Pam was surprised at first. The account I shared matched Jason's story. Stacey became more involved in our conversation at that point. She told us how much what he had overheard had affected Jason's life. She said the two of them had talked about it often over the years.

Stacey also shared that up to the time Jason over-heard their dad's conversation, they had never heard about a murder case or her father's involvement in anything like it. They had just been kids. Stacey said Jason had told her right away and she had asked him to be quiet about it because it was their father and didn't think they should tell on him.

She knew Jason told his mom after the death of their father. Hearing the truth about what had happened solidified both Pam and Stacey's belief in Jason's account.

After leaving Pam's house, Stacey came with us to meet up with Donna to talk to Janice. Janice was apprehensive at first, but she soon admitted that Pete hadn't come home after dropping off the pizzas at the party with Jeff. At the time, Janice thought Pete had stayed out partying all night with Scott. She told us she testified at the trial what Pete told her to say, which was that Pete left the party and came home, spending the rest of the night with her.

Other witnesses had testified that Pete had left the party shortly after delivering pizzas. If he didn't go home, where did he go?

Janice was not willing to put anything in writing or help us, at that time, as she was afraid of perjury charges. She also shared that she remembered they had been missing a hammer from their home after the murder.

Our last stop was to meet with Scott. Donna and Stacey accompanied us again. Donna hadn't been able to reach Scott beforehand, and we surprised him. He was unwilling to answer any questions that day but said if we made an appointment he would talk to someone about what he knew.

At the end of our interviews that day, and as we were driving away, Mike shared that in his observations, nothing we learned that day pointed to Jeff as having committed this crime but did lead to Pete. He became a believer and advocate for Jeff.

—ⱱ—

The very next day, Scott met with Jean, who was still helping with the case. Scott hadn't had any contact with Jeff since the morning of March 6, 1981, but he was willing to share what he knew and remembered.

Even after so many years, Scott could account for the approximate timing and Jeff's whereabouts the night and morning they had been partying. He could also confirm the fact that he and Jeff had cooked a meal when they came home, watched TV, and that Jeff had gone to sleep on a couch in the living room at Pete's place, where he was also staying. He remembered seeing Jeff still asleep in the same spot when he got up to go to work just a few hours later. He also remembered Jeff giving him a key to his place before he left town that afternoon.

Scott would also attest that the following morning, Pete brought together people who had been partying with Jeff and Scott the night before. He said Pete told them they could all be in trouble and said they needed to get their stories straight. He asked Scott to tell police he knew Jeff had killed his roommate. Scott refused because the tale Pete was putting together did not match up with what he knew had happened since he had been with Jeff the entire night.

In his interview with Jean, Scott said that he didn't know Jeff very well (Jeff said they met in treatment) but that he had known Pete most of his life and he was like a brother to him. But still, he didn't want to lie for Pete. Not wanting to make Pete mad, Scott moved to Colorado where he had family, so he wouldn't have to testify. Pete knew where he had gone and why.

Scott said he had felt it was strange that Pete got involved—it seemed out of character. Pete never told Scott he was the one who killed Jeff's roommate, but after Pete's death, he started hearing people say Pete had told them he had. He'd also talked to Jason about what Jason had overheard his father say.

Scott said he was willing to come to court to testify to everything he had said. The habeas hearing was scheduled for the following week.

All of this led me to fully believe Jeff's story.

CHAPTER 20

JEFF'S LAST DAY IN COURT

One week later, twelve years after his initial application for a writ of habeas corpus, Jeff's long-awaited day in court arrived, June 18, 1996. Martin felt it was a good case. We were all hopeful that this would finally lead to Jeff's freedom. By this time, Jeff had spent more than fifteen years behind bars.

Jeff arrived in his orange jumpsuit. He was chained at the waist, with a chain attached to the shackles on his ankles. His wrists were restrained in a black box. I was stunned at the sight of him like this. It's extremely difficult to see a person you love bound and chained like a dangerous animal. They removed them during the hearing, but I still felt sick to my stomach.

Jeff was used to it though and happy to finally have this day arrive. We were permitted to pray together before the hearing. Jeff entered the courtroom, and we took our seats behind him in the gallery, where spectators can watch court proceedings.

During his trial in 1981, Jeff had no one there for him. This time, besides myself, his friend Roger, and a friend who visited Jeff regularly through the M-2 Program[4] were also present. Our presence deeply moved Jeff. His life had changed so much since first arriving at the prison in 1981. One significant change had been allowing others into authentic relationships with him. He expressed his heartfelt gratitude to each one of us.

Before the actual hearing, the judge and attorneys held a motion hearing. The state's attorney had asked for dismissal of the habeas. There were five points addressed. Two of those points concerned key people in the writ of habeas corpus that referenced people who had died. The judge decided the state was prejudiced "by having issues involving dead people and people who can't testify." The issue included any testimony that involved Pete, the affidavits from people to whom he had admitted his guilt, and Jason, Pete's son.

Scott arrived to tell his story about what had happened—what he felt he should have testified to at Jeff's original trial. When it came to his turn, Scott explained why he did not testify in court initially—because he had suspicions about Pete's involvement and Pete orchestrating other people's testimony, including trying to coerce him (Scott) to testify against Jeff. Scott also wanted to tell about Jason's confession of what he overheard his father say since Jason had confided in him. Scott tried different ways to say what he had come to share,

---

4   "M-2 stands for Man-to-Man visitation on a one-to-one, friend-to-friend basis with a prison inmate at the South Dakota State Penitentiary." From brochure from M-2 Office, Sioux Falls, SD.

but much of what he had to tell, the judge barred him from speaking about as it involved Pete or Jason. He was only allowed to answer questions about his time with Jeff that evening and the timeline as much as he could recall. The state's attorney for the habeas had extensive experience in the courtroom. Jeff's attorney, while not as experienced, made a valiant effort to share how Jeff had been under- and misrepresented in his trial by information not being shared, incompetency of Jeff's trial attorney, and overzealousness of the prosecution. Both the original trial's state's attorney and Jeff's defense attorney testified. Jeff's attorney was no longer practicing law and said he had always believed in Jeff's innocence but didn't remember much, and since he was no longer practicing, he didn't have his files to review. The former state's attorney said he didn't remember much about the case either.

To the judge, it mainly came down to Scott's testimony being fifteen years too late, and Jeff's original attorney's trial strategy. He said it made sense to him how things were handled based on the attorney's strategy.

The judge issued an order denying Jeff's Writ of Habeas Corpus. The State said it, "Has been unduly prejudiced in its ability to respond to Jeff's Application of Writ of Habeas Corpus" because it had been delayed past five years.

However, the decision of the judge to deny the habeas was not a total surprise. Martin informed us that whichever side lost that day, would be appealing the decision to the South Dakota Supreme Court. We had hoped for a win as a vote of confidence but did not lose hope with the results of the hearing. Martin assured us he would file the appeal. And he did.

A couple of months after Martin had filed the appeal with the Supreme Court, I received a call from him. It was apparent he was distraught. He let us know that while he had filed the appeal, he had not known about recent changes in the law regarding the timeline to do so. The appeal had been filed one day late, and the State Supreme Court had dismissed it. Martin appealed their decision, sighting it was not Jeff's fault and asked for the habeas to be reinstated, but this appeal was also denied.

Martin left his firm, and another attorney was assigned to Jeff's case. The last resort for relief in the court system would be at the federal level, the U.S. District Court. Jeff filed to have his habeas heard at the federal level, but it was also denied. The reason given was that procedurally it could not be acted upon because the state's Supreme Court habeas was not timely.

On March 16, 1998, the United States District Court, entered a judgment, denying Jeff's writ of habeas corpus. All Jeff's legal remedies through the court system had been exhausted.

CHAPTER 21

TWO BECOME ONE

The few months before the federal court's decision had been an exciting time for Jeff and me. Late in the Fall of 1997, after much prayer, I felt God's peace about marrying Jeff.

After backing out of our earlier marriage plans, I had tried to keep our relationship on the level of friendship. Even when I knew I still loved Jeff, I believed there was no reason to marry when we didn't know if we'd ever have a life together on the outside.

But, we'd been through a lot over the years, and our relationship had matured. I was close to finishing my undergraduate degree, and my children were grown and mostly out of the house.

I wondered if our marriage could be "real" and had even been told by a pastor or two that it wouldn't be a real marriage because we could not come together "as one."

I prayed and sought God. Would our love for each other be enough to sustain a marriage like this? Could what we have be enough if this was all we ever had—two visits a week, a brief kiss, holding hands, sitting side by side? I also knew it had to be my decision. I knew Jeff wanted our marriage, but he wasn't going to push it and probably wouldn't ask me again.

I prayed and prayed. I knew if we married, God would be there for us. My hesitation was whether I could withstand the loneliness of not having my husband by my side. Over time, it felt like I had God's blessing and peace descended over me.

I was ready to bring it up to Jeff when he called one day, with a shaky voice.

Up to this time, he still lived in Sioux Falls, mere minutes from where I lived. Visiting options made it easy to see him on a regular basis. We'd heard rumors the prison system was considering bringing lifers back to the facility in Springfield, South Dakota. It was now a male-only prison.

Jeff and I had had several discussions about the rumors and what he would do should the opportunity arise for him to go back. I had voiced my concerns about making the two-hour drive with my limited funds and not-so-reliable vehicle. We'd agreed that if given the option and a choice in the matter, Jeff would opt to stay in Sioux Falls.

But, when presented with the chance to be one of the first lifers to return to Springfield, it had been too tempting for him, and he'd said yes. He would be leaving any day.

On top of the two-hour drive each way, visiting hours were restricted to weekends. The bottom fell out of my marriage plans.

On some level, I understood why Jeff said yes to moving back. I knew he missed being in Springfield. The facility, having been built as a college campus, housed the inmates in dorm rooms, not traditional cells. Also, they were not locked into their rooms by officers in a control room. They could let themselves in and out at will most of the time. There was more freedom of movement inside and outside, and the windows in their rooms opened to the outside air.

At that time, there was less staff turnover than in Sioux Falls. During his previous six and a half years in Springfield, he was well-known by staff and was treated with more respect, something he dearly missed.

Jeff transferred to Springfield in December of 1997.

It only took a couple of weekend visits for me to fully understand why he needed this change, especially after all he'd recently been through with his case. I noticed his relaxed demeanor and personally experienced the respect he appreciated when I was greeted warmly by the staff, as Jeff's girlfriend.

At our second visit, I asked Jeff if he still wanted to get married. It had been a little over four years since we met. He almost fell out of his chair from shock and had a huge smile on his face as he answered, "Yes!"

The prison picked our wedding date, Friday the 13th in March of 1998. It was a perfect date for me. I am terrible at remembering important dates. I would have a husband with a New Year's Eve birthday and a Friday the 13th anniversary date. I felt God smiling at me with these seemingly minor details.

It also reframed March 13 for Jeff. Before, this date was etched in his memory as the date when he had learned he was a murder suspect. Now it was a day to celebrate something beautiful.

Weddings in prison are simple affairs and held in or near the visiting room. On March 13, 1998, it was lightly snowing as I made the drive to Springfield with two friends and my three sons. I was nervous and missed the turn-off. But, we still arrived in plenty of time.

Weddings at the prison typically are officiated by people previously unknown to the couple, and often not clergy. We were blessed to be married by a pastor who knew both of us, and who supported our marriage. I cannot tell you how much that meant to us.

Our wedding was performed in a small room off the visiting area and lasted less than 20 minutes. No pictures, music, cake, or fancy dress. But, it was meaningful in its simplicity. We wrote our vows to each other. It was a sweet time and memorable in all the right ways.

People often ask why I married Jeff when we may never be together. It is a complicated answer in some ways. But it's also simple. I knew I was going to love Jeff for as long as we were on earth; and I wanted him to know that I wasn't going anywhere—that he could count on me. In the end, isn't that what marriage is about?

Many newlyweds know that they may face challenging situations in their marriage, but they don't know if or what they'll be. We already had a pretty good idea of what those would be for us and could make the commitment knowing that up front.

Looking back now, I believe God knew the decision I would make, even though it was my choice. I could feel His smile on me as we both remembered my earnest prayer in 1990. Being, "Totally dependent on You" has a special meaning when your husband is locked up.

CHAPTER 22

NEXT STEPS

Days after our wedding, we would learn of the federal court's decision and that there were no more legal avenues through the court system for Jeff's wrongful conviction. But an even tougher event took place one month later.

I made one of the hardest phone calls ever. I called the prison to ask someone to have Jeff call me back so I could give him the news that his best friend had died suddenly of a brain aneurysm.

Roger had been released in 1994. In November that same year, he had married Jonette, someone he had known before going to prison. They bought a house in Sioux Falls and settled into married life. Roger was helping to raise Jonette's young daughter, and things were going well for them.

In early 1998, Jonette gave birth to a beautiful baby girl. When she was just two months old, Roger got up in the night to feed her. He had just handed the baby back to Jonette when he told her that he didn't feel right. He slumped down and when Jonette came to him, he was already gone.

When I told Jeff what had happened, he could hardly speak. His voice was raw with emotion as he thanked me and said he'd call again later. Roger was the first person that Jeff had truly let into his life, and their love and respect for each other were genuine. The loss was tremendous.

Jeff was asked to write a eulogy, as Roger's closest friend. Since Jeff couldn't be present, I read his eulogy to the crowd gathered. Jeff expressed the deep bond between them and his gratitude for their friendship continuing even after Roger left prison.

While Roger was alive, he had made some contacts on Jeff's behalf. There was talk that if Jeff would admit guilt, there was a possibility his sentence could be commuted from life without parole to some number of years so he would be eligible for parole at some point. A similar arrangement had recently been offered to a woman lifer who had maintained her innocence. The insinuation was that Jeff could have the same deal if he would confess to the murder. All of this talk came through Roger's contacts—not anyone we knew.

Roger had asked me to present the possibility to Jeff. Jeff didn't hesitate and said "No! I used to be a liar and a thief, and I am not going back to being either of those. God will have to get me out based on telling the truth." He has never wavered on that decision over the years.

I finished my bachelor's degree at the end of 1997 and eight months later, started working toward my master's degree in social work. I'd become disillusioned with our criminal justice system and no longer had any desire to pursue a degree in law.

For me, truth and justice should go hand in hand. I'd learned that what the former judge had told me in those early days had been correct. The truth didn't matter after a conviction. It didn't seem that not having a fair trial mattered either. I wanted nothing to do with this seemingly unjust system.

Even with the challenges facing us, we enjoyed our married life. While traveling to Springfield was difficult, and their visitation system was (and still is) hard on families, we settled in and prayed about what to do next. It would again be a few years before anything happened.

Now that there were no options in the court system, Jeff could begin applying to the Board of Pardons and Paroles (board) again for a commutation, a reduction in his sentence. Occasionally, lifers had been granted a reduction from life-without-parole to a number-of-years, making them eligible to appear before the parole board for a possible release. A commutation by the board was now Jeff's only option in his quest for freedom.

A hearing before the board cannot be applied for when a legal case is pending. Jeff had submitted his first application for a commutation in September 1986, five years into his incarceration. He was granted a hearing for the following month. Jeff had been working hard to turn his life around in the previous months. He'd quit drinking and using and had been granted inside/outside trustee status. He went to the hearing hopeful.

As Jeff remembers it, the first question asked of him at the hearing was "Why did you do it?" He answered that he hadn't done it. There wasn't much to say after that. He received word within days that his request for commutation was "Denied."

Jeff later learned that one of the key things the board is looking for is acceptance of responsibility for the crime committed and a heart attitude of remorse.

It makes sense in almost every other case. But, Jeff couldn't give them what they wanted.

For a few years he worked on filing the Writ of Habeas Corpus and let the commutation requests rest while seeing that through. The system does not allow both processes to continue simultaneously.

He applied again in 1992 and 1993 and was denied a hearing both times. Between 1994 and 1996, he had an active habeas case again and so didn't file those years.

In 1997, he had been denied his state habeas and hadn't yet filed his Federal habeas, so applied for a hearing. Again, he received notice: "Denied."

After his federal habeas denial in 1998, Jeff began applying for a commutation hearing again. He applied in 1999, 2000, 2001 and 2002. Each time he was denied.

In December 2002, Jeff personally appealed to then Governor Bill Janklow who would soon be leaving office. Jeff had written before, pleading his case, but he'd never had a reply. Now was his final chance. On January 4, 2003, Jeff received a letter stating: "As my fourth term as governor comes to a close I find that more and more of my correspondence deals with things that, regrettably, I will be unable to address during my remaining days in office. The time I have left in office doesn't allow me to give the necessary consideration to your request."

He went on to say that Jeff should send any future correspondence to the incoming governor, Michael Rounds, as he, "Wouldn't presume to share" Jeff's letter with him. Governor Bill Janklow was leaving his governorship for a new role in Washington, D.C. having won the election as our state's lone Representative.

—◊◊—

Every application to the board after 1986 met with the same response: "After carefully considering your Application for (Pardon/Commutation of Sentence) the Action of the Board is as follows: 'Denied.'"

When Jeff wrote and asked for the reason for denial, the response was, "The Board does not give reasons for denial." While left to speculate as to the reason for the denials, Jeff assumed it was because of his claim of innocence.

Jeff spent many a night on his knees after these rejections, crying out to God and asking "Why?" He read the Bible where it says God frees the prisoner, executes justice for the oppressed, is merciful, etc. It was hard to accept having to do more time for a crime he didn't do. He knew freedom in his heart—but he was ready to experience physical freedom outside the prison walls. Each denial felt like a kick in the gut. And yet, each time, God gave him the strength, faith, and perseverance to not give up and to continue to trust Him.

—∽—

In 2000, a friend of mine who was a teacher at the prison asked me to meet with a friend of hers. Cheri's husband at the time was soon to enter the South Dakota prison system. Cheri had questions about what it was like to visit and be married to someone in prison.

We discovered we were both social workers and shared a heart for social justice issues. I shared what I knew and hoped it would be helpful on the difficult journey she was about to experience.

It would be months before we ran into each other again. Soon after sentencing, Cheri's husband was sent to Springfield and ended up rooming with Jeff. Cheri and I became casual acquaintances since we saw each other on weekends when she came with her children for visits.

One day, Cheri approached me saying she was planning to go to law school and wanted to know more about Jeff's case. Apparently, Jeff had shared his story with her husband, who then shared it with his wife.

We arranged a meeting where I shared details of Jeff's story. Cheri said that one of her primary motives for going to law school was to help people like Jeff, and she would like to take on Jeff's case when she got her degree. Shortly after this meeting, Jeff was transferred back to Sioux Falls, and we lost touch for a season.

In the fall of 2003, I received a call from Cheri, now in her 2nd year of law school. She hadn't forgotten Jeff's plight and asked if I could bring Jeff's paperwork for her and her classmates to look over. I copied the files and dropped them off at her house, not knowing what to expect. I met her friends, and classmates, Jan, Bryan, and Matt.

They were eager to dive in and help if they could. It was encouraging to Jeff and me, although I had doubts about what they could do since our understanding was that we had no more legal remedies left. Still, they were hopeful, and that was refreshing. We had both felt so alone in the quest for Jeff's freedom, and it did both our hearts good to have people care and join us.

After they'd had time to look over the paperwork, we met again. Cheri, Jan, Bryan, and Matt were inclined to believe Jeff had been wrongfully convicted and decided to work on his case outside of their class work.

Bryan was a third-year student and had begun an externship with the Public Defender's Office. He had the opportunity to review Jeff's case with attorneys experienced in criminal law and ask for input and advice.

After realizing all legal remedies through the courts had truly been exhausted, the students set about helping Jeff get a commutation hearing before the Board of Pardons and Paroles. It was a long-shot. But, the students hoped that with their help, Jeff would finally be granted a hearing. They planned to present a case and belief in his wrongful conviction before the board.

In January 2004, Jeff applied once again. But this time, a letter from the law students, along with a legal memorandum and paperwork to back up their position, accompanied his application.

CHAPTER 23

HEART ATTACK

February 9, 2004, began like any other day for Jeff. He had breakfast and returned to his cell to wait until his time to go to work.

He worked for the prison as a chapel orderly, making twenty-five cents an hour. Right on time that morning, his door popped open at 7:30 a.m., and he went upstairs to begin the day's duties. He and a fellow chapel orderly would be carrying boxes of books from the chaplain's office to the prison chapel.

About ten minutes later, Jeff was discovered by his co-worker on the landing by the stairs and appeared to be having a seizure. His co-worker notified their supervisor. She called the code right away. The response was fast, and officers found he had no heartbeat and was not breathing. They started CPR immediately.

Soon, the first responding officers were joined by others in the effort to revive Jeff. Someone was sent to bring defibrillator paddles from another building, and someone else called 911. Responders would use the paddles three times to get his heart started—twice before transporting him and once on the way to the hospital.

I was getting out of the shower and saw a light blinking on my phone. An officer at the prison had left a message that Jeff was on the way to the hospital. His message didn't give much detail, only to call the hospital to find out Jeff's condition and to call the Captain on duty, for permission, if I wanted to see Jeff.

I called the hospital and talked to an officer who advised me to get permission right away to visit as his condition seemed grave. I would later learn he was the first person to perform CPR, saving Jeff's life.

My whole body shook as I got dressed and called the prison to obtain permission to see him. I also called my mom to ask for prayer.

I arrived at the emergency room area of the hospital shortly after Jeff had arrived. The pastor of the church Jeff attended was present and greeted me. An officer came to take me back to the room where Jeff was.

He had a breathing tube, IVs, a catheter, and light blanket covering his mid-section. I had never seen so much of him—even after almost six years of marriage. It was surreal on many levels.

They had placed him in a coma. He lay eerily still and entirely unresponsive to my touch. My husband— the man who had always greeted me with a smile, a twinkle in his eyes, and a reassuring hug and squeeze. He looked so big and still lying there.

The doctors were trying to figure out what had happened to him, which is why they induced a coma. He would remain that way for a couple of days.

In addition to the officers in the crowded room, in accordance with prison protocol, Jeff was chained to the bed. One hand to a side rail and one ankle to the foot rail. It broke my heart.

I remember praying on the way to the hospital, "Lord, I know Jeff is your child and if you have to take him home, I'll try to understand. I know I'll still love you. I'd really like him to stay here though."

Looking at my husband, lying motionless, in the emergency room, I wanted him to live more than anything.

Doctors asked about Jeff's family medical history. I knew his father had experienced a brain aneurysm and that his mother and one sister had both died from heart attacks. That was all I knew, and the doctor said both were possibilities in Jeff's case.

They planned to run tests and asked me to find out any more family history that I could. The prison granted permission for me to visit if it was okay with the hospital staff. It was, and I hardly left Jeff's side for the next three days.

As scary as this time was, it was also the first time I experienced treatment as a "real" wife. Hospital staff, including doctors, talked to me about my husband's medical condition. They told me how he was doing and shared test results.

His attending physician even asked if I had any other health concerns for him I'd like checked out while he was there. I pointed out that I was not permitted to make any decisions on Jeff's behalf. The doctor's response was as far as he was concerned, I had all the rights of any other spouse.

I'd been told in the past, by prison staff, that even though Jeff and I were married, he was in their custody and control. I had no rights.

I didn't abuse my "rights" at the hospital, but it was affirming and unique to our situation, to matter in

Jeff's treatment. I was as much in the loop as I'm sure the prison was.

It was also a special time as I spoke with the correctional officers who came to stand guard over Jeff, some who'd known him longer than I had. Sometimes there was just one officer, and we would chat. It's hard to explain, but it felt normal.

Families are often viewed suspiciously, especially wives and girlfriends. Apparently, we are considered more easily coerced to do illegal things for the inmates. Who knew?

After a couple of days, medical staff hadn't determined the cause of Jeff's medical issues but did feel it was safe to let him regain consciousness. It would be another full day before he would come out of the fog and aware of what was happening and why.

It was an emotional time for Jeff, realizing all that had happened to him, and that God still had plans for his life. He was able to thank the officers who had responded so quickly to save his life.

Valentine's Day arrived in the middle of his stay, and in true Jeff-thoughtfulness, he had a friend buy a card he could sign and present to me. He was enjoying all the extra time we had together. It's not like that anymore when an inmate is in the hospital. We both appreciate the memories from this unique time, on top of the fact that Jeff is still here to tell about it.

Jeff also enjoyed the perk of being able to choose his meals when he was able to have regular food again. Hospital food might not be to everyone's liking, but Jeff enjoyed the variety of meat, fruits, and vegetables, which are very limited at inside prison walls. There were other things on the menu that just are not available in prison—and he tried it all (except cooked peas and carrots!)

The warden visited a couple of times and remarked that it isn't often someone makes it through that type of heart attack at the prison. Jeff had what is called a "silent" heart attack. There was no warning. He only felt a little woozy and remembers starting to sit down on a step before waking up in the hospital a few days later.

Ten minutes earlier the morning of February 9th, Jeff would have still been locked up. God only knows when someone would have discovered him unconscious in his cell. We felt blessed by the timing and by the staff's early intervention. We knew our story wasn't over.

Eventually, the doctors found the cause, a blocked artery. They put a stent in his heart, and he was returned to the prison just over a week after having arrived. Jeff received doctor's orders to have a heart-healthy diet and physical therapy. The heart-healthy diet doesn't exist in prison where carbs, processed meat, and the occasional overcooked vegetables are the norm. But, he took part in physical therapy at a local rehab center. For that, we were grateful again.

Jeff made a full recovery in time to be part of the process unfolding with the law students and Board of Pardons and Paroles.

CHAPTER 24

COMMUTATION HEARING, FINALLY

While Jeff was still in the hospital, Cheri, Jan, Bryan, and Matt had received notice that the Board of Pardons and Paroles wanted a meeting with them to discuss their involvement with Jeff's commutation request.

Evidently, this situation was not typical—an inmate so adamantly claiming innocence before the board, nor a group of law students, who have their whole careers before them, arguing the innocence of such a man.

The meeting with the law students and members of the board took place on February 26th. The next day, Jeff learned he was granted a hearing.

The board advised the students to have everyone possible present to back up their case. They certainly had their work cut out for them.

The board scheduled the hearing for May 16th.

Lifers requesting a commutation of their sentence are required to meet with all nine members of the board for their hearing.

May 16, 2004, finally arrived, and it is questionable as to who was more nervous.

The law students were presenting their "first case" after months of preparation. They had no courtroom experience at this point, so this was new and exciting for them.

I was a bundle of nerves, even though surrounded by family and friends. Jeff now had many more supporters, and quite a few showed up for his hearing: Martin, our former attorney was present, some family members and friends, the pastor who had married us, and a couple of former inmates who had known Jeff from the inside. So much work had gone into getting to this point, and it was hard to believe the day had finally arrived.

Jeff was nervous, but he also seemed the most at peace. He made the sweetest gesture, having a friend of his bring me a dozen roses before the hearing. He wanted me to know how much he loved me for standing by him and helping to get to this day.

Stacey, Jason's sister and Pete's daughter, delayed a vacation trip to the shores of South Carolina with her family and drove from her home in Wichita, Kansas, to South Dakota to share her and her brother's experience and what she believed to be true.

Others present when we arrived at the room, included the nine board members, a couple of staff from the parole board office, two correctional officers, and Jeff. I was offered a seat at the table, next to Jeff, and we held hands during most of the hearing. The room was packed full of people, and anticipation.

One of the board members knew Jeff from his past, even before prison. He asked Jeff if he should recuse himself because of this past relationship. Jeff told him he didn't need to because if he knew him back then, he would be able to see that he's no longer the same person.

—ᴍ—

When Jeff gets emotional, his hands get sweaty. Since we were holding hands, it was easy for me to gauge how he was feeling. He kept squeezing my hand as people spoke on his behalf.

Martin, his former habeas attorney, addressed the board as did a former inmate who shared Jeff's impact on his life, even after his release. Others spoke a few words and then it was time for the law students to present.

They presented Jeff's case and what had taken place since his trial. They also brought three witnesses to the hearing.

Stacey shared why she felt it was important enough for her to drive all the way from Wichita, Kansas, and take time away from her vacation to testify at this hearing.

Stacey shared about her brother Jason's admission to her when they were children. She shared about their upbringing and how you didn't tell on people, especially not your own father. At the time, she had asked Jason to be quiet. But, she knew Jason was telling the truth.

She tearfully conveyed to the board that she loved her father, but they had grown up knowing what he was capable of. Stacey told them how she and Jason had often talked about what he had overheard, feeling sorry that another man was in prison for something their father did. She believed this knowledge had profoundly impacted Jason and helped lead to Jason's problems with drugs and eventual suicide.

Stacey shared how important it was to her to make this right. She believed that deep down, her father wanted this too. (It is a deep-seated burden to her even to this day.)

Also, present by phone were Rick, to whom Pete had confessed to the day after the murder, and Bob, Jeff's friend from Georgia who now lived in New Jersey.

Except for the letter written to Jeff in 1983 after Pete's death, Rick had not had any contact with Jeff since before the murder. Rick handwrote his letter while in prison in Terra Haute, Indiana but had since gotten his life together. He now lived in Arizona and owned an auto mechanic shop. Rick stood by his story and earlier affidavit that Pete had admitted to him that he had killed Jeff's roommate.

Bob also stood by his deposition given to Martin in 1996. He reiterated Jeff's plan to come to Georgia and Jeff's lack of concern that the police were looking for him when he arrived at Bob's March 12, 1981. Bob had still not had any contact with Jeff since that day.

Both expressed their surprise at Jeff's continued incarceration.

Jeff became emotional during both Rick and Bob's testimony. Except for Scott's limited testimony at the habeas hearing, no one had testified on his behalf for his case. It was also the first time he'd heard his friend Bob's voice since the day of his arrest more than twenty-three years before.

After the students finished presenting, one of the board members turned his attention to Jeff and began to ask questions. At one point, he asked if anyone who knew Jeff since entering the prison and could tell the board how he has done and was living life on the inside. At first, there was silence. Staff at the penitentiary are forbidden to testify on an inmate's behalf at hearings.

After a short silence, the Executive Director of the Board of Pardons and Paroles spoke up saying he believed he was allowed to speak since he was no longer on staff at the prison. Jeff's hand squeezed mine, knowing this man had known him since he had arrived in prison and knew Jeff before he changed. He didn't know what to expect.

The Director went on to say he'd known Jeff since his early days in prison and had seen many changes. It was encouraging to the board members who wanted to make their decision based on the whole picture. When he finished sharing, a few more questions came up for Jeff.

Finally satisfied, the board member leading the questioning, looked around the table at the other board members and said he'd like to make a recommendation. He recommended that Jeff's sentence be commuted from life-without-parole to "a number of years to be determined." The board voted unanimously in favor of the recommendation. The final decision rested with the governor. We thought it would only be a formality. Why wouldn't he go along with the board who had done its homework?

We were ecstatic! I think everyone in the room was moved and there were tears, hugs, and hopefulness.

Prison staff let Jeff say thank you to each guest, some of whom he was meeting for the first time. He was deeply affected by each person's presence on his behalf.

It was hard to say goodbye to Jeff when the last person left. It would have been nice to savor this moment in time, together. We were full of hope, even though we didn't know what number of years they would recommend for his sentence reduction.

The hearing was Friday afternoon, and we had a visit planned for the next morning.

Thankfully, we didn't have long to wait. Jeff received a notice from the board shortly before our visit. Their recommendation was for a sentence reduction from life-without-parole to ninety years and six months.

Now, that might seem a little excessive still, but sentencing guidelines were different when Jeff came to prison in 1981, and he was still under those rules. Back then, you earned "good time" for good behavior. Jeff had been on good behavior for a long time.

Typically the sentence would be rounded off to a whole number. The additional "six months" was puzzling until we discovered its intention.

The board had figured the earliest possible time for Jeff to come before them if the governor acted promptly, as they expected him to do. If everything went as planned and the governor approved the recommendation, Jeff could come before them in July. It was possible they could parole Jeff in just two months!

We couldn't have been more hopeful. We don't know what the board believed about Jeff's innocence. But nine people, specifically appointed to fill the role of determining if a person is capable and should be released back into society, were united in their belief that Jeff deserved that opportunity. They did their job, examined the information, asked questions, and thoughtfully and carefully made their recommendation to the governor.

We dared to dream again.

CHAPTER 25

BACK TO WAITING

We talked about what the day would look like when he was released. Would I pick him up at the prison alone? What should we do first? Go home? Shop for clothes? Cook and eat a meal together? See loved ones?

We talked about spending time with family. Jeff dreamed that maybe his son would eventually want to know him, and they could go fishing together. He imagined spending time outdoors, listening to nature and walking barefoot on the earth. Jeff talked a lot about food—food he missed and recipes his mom made when he was growing up.

He talked about the type of work he'd like to do and people he'd like to help. We talked about what church we wanted to attend together. He dreamed of spending time with his dad and taking him out of the nursing home and going fishing. They had made their peace over the years—both having changed.

We talked about what our marriage would look like and the changes to our relationship. I'd lived alone for many years, and Jeff had lived in an institution for almost a quarter of a century. We knew there would be challenges and talked at great length about those. We talked about support both of us would need as we adjusted.

We thanked God for all the pieces that seemed to be falling into place and how much we would need to depend on Him to help us adjust to this new life together.

We waited for the governor's much-anticipated answer.

Weeks went by. July came and went. We adjusted our expectations and hoped for a Christmas miracle, or maybe it would be at the end of the year.

Through letters, we pleaded with the governor. We only received form letters, like the one dated June 22, 2004, "The determination to commute your sentence will be based partially on the information provided to me from the Board of Pardons and Paroles and my own determination. To date, I have not made this determination, but I will let you know when I do."

Christmas 2004 came and went; as did Christmas 2005.

The governor was running for re-election in 2006. We hoped that after the election was over, he might consider the board's recommendation. But the years dragged on with no response to our continued efforts to elicit a decision.

A friend spearheaded a yellow postcard campaign in 2005. Hundreds of bright yellow postcards poured into the governor's office.

They said "Dear Governor Rounds, What about Jeff Howard? We care." Then it had a place for the sender's name, address, and signature.

Postcards came from across the United States and even a few from people in other countries, who knew our story. During this time, numerous letters went to the governor in support of Jeff's freedom, referencing the board's recommendation. The only responses received were letters saying a decision had not yet been reached. The governor refused to meet with anyone regarding the case. We were only informed it was "still on his desk," whatever that meant. We were entirely in the dark.

In 2008, the local newspaper reported that two members of the Board of Pardons and Paroles resigned their positions out of frustration concerning the inaction of the governor on several of the board's recommendations. It had been more than four years since the board's recommendation on Jeff's case. The governor's explanation was that sometimes he must deliberate longer than other people might. According to the newspaper report, out of 202 recommendations made since 2003, 141 had been approved, and 23 denied. That left 38 people's lives hanging in the balance, waiting for a decision.[5] Most of those he had decided on were minor violations where people were asking for pardons to clear their names

The years dragged on, and we suspected no decision was likely before the governor's last days in office at the end of his second term. And that's what happened.

---

5   Ruckman, P.S., Jr. "South Dakota: Pardon Us. We're Otta Here." PardonPower.com. http://www.pardonpower.com/2008/10/south-dakota-pardon-us-were-otta-here.html (accessed June 7, 2018).

CHAPTER 26

THE HARDEST DAY

As the end of Governor Mike Round's second term drew near, our anticipation grew.

We wrote letters, as did many who supported Jeff's freedom. One of the law students, Cheri, now an attorney, attempted to contact the governor or his staff again.

We began hearing of decisions on other lifers who were also waiting. Two received their commutation, but no word came out about Jeff. Cheri had contact with a staff member close to the governor and was able to glean a little information. He told her it was on the governor's desk and still being considered.

One of the commutations decided on by the governor had drawn public criticism. The victim's family had inadvertently not been notified and was upset, making it known that they didn't agree with the governor's decision. The story made headlines. We worried it might impact the governor's decision on Jeff's request.

At the same time, the victim's family in Jeff's case had been notified and had started a campaign against Jeff's freedom. Most of them resided out of state, but there were a few in South Dakota. They sent an online petition to the governor. Their campaign hadn't made the news, and we didn't know how much this might influence his decision.

Governor Rounds' last full day in office would be Friday, January 7, 2011. It was a couple of days out, and Jeff's commutation was the only one left undecided. An active prayer group was organized at a local church where some friends of ours attended and were on staff.

Thursday afternoon, I received a call about 3:00 p.m., from a man Jeff knew and I had met, who had previously worked as a supervisor where Jeff worked. He was an outsider. He had received a call from one of the current ministry staff members who, as they were leaving the prison through the front lobby, heard prison officers talking about cleaning up the area as the governor was on his way to visit the prison.

It seemed odd that the governor would be coming to the prison the day before his last day in office. In South Dakota, the governor's office is in Pierre, about four and a half hours' drive from Sioux Falls, where the prison is.

I sent a text to our friends at the church who were praying. A short time later, it was communicated that one of their church staff, who had lobbied for two years under this governor a few years earlier, said if the governor went to the prison on his last days in office, it would be to grant a pardon.

You can only imagine what was going through our minds. I let Cheri know, and she made some calls but couldn't find out anything. All we could do was wait.

Friday morning came. We received confirmation the governor had indeed come and gone from the prison the day before, but still no word on his decision. My son and his wife had planned to visit Jeff that afternoon and so went to the 12:30 visit while I waited for news.

I made several calls and texts to Cheri, but she wasn't responding, which I felt was odd. A feeling began growing in the pit of my stomach, but I still hung onto the hope the governor would commute Jeff's sentence. Why would he take so long, only to deny him?

Mid-afternoon, Cheri called with the news—Governor Rounds had denied the board's recommendation. She had been informed earlier that day but was directed not to tell me.

After more than six and a half years of waiting, it was over. I cannot even begin to express the pain in my heart. And, even worse, after talking to my son, I learned Jeff did not know. He would be calling later that evening, and it looked like I would be the one who had to give him the devastating news.

I fell to my knees, before God, utterly broken. The truth was on our side. God, how could you let this happen? Why didn't you hear our cries? Why can't justice prevail? How could you let the governor make this decision? Don't you control everything?

The grief was overwhelming! My heart broke for Jeff. For almost thirty years he had endured this unfathomable injustice: living in a cage where his movements are restricted, and decisions made without regard to individual needs.

He'd missed out on family milestones, relationships with his kids, nieces, and nephews, spending time with family. He'd had to watch life moving on in their worlds, without him.

He'd missed out on experiencing the outdoors in ways he so longed for—fishing, hunting, and watching the seasons unfold. He missed shoveling snow, working in the fields, and the satisfaction of planting and harvesting.

He'd already missed thirty years of life on the outside. Why could this not have ended right now? Why wasn't he walking into our home—a free man?

I longed for the type of marriage where two people have the day-to-day intimacy of being truly known by another person and yet, still loved. I am married but live alone. I long for the comfort of my husband's arms around me when I am wounded by the world, to share my joys as well as my trials in real time, not having to wait days until our next visit. I long for his sweet kisses. I long to share life together.

The anguish overwhelmed me. I was alone when I got the news, and I let it wash over me. I poured out my heart to God. I asked God, "Don't you care about us?" I questioned: "What have I done or not done? What are we missing? How could you not want the glory of letting Jeff be free?"

One of the things that hit hardest was the reaction of the people who did not want to see Jeff freed. They felt *they* had won and God had been on *their* side. They were jubilant that God had answered their prayers. God could not answer both our prayers. Why were their prayers answered and not ours? How would they have felt if it had gone the other way?

When Jeff called that evening, I broke the news to him. His voice was quiet and shaky. He had suspected this would be the answer after the others received their commutation and he hadn't. Still, he knew his case was different and had hoped for his freedom. When the day had come and gone with no word, he knew deep down he was being denied.

Still, hearing it as a reality was a blow. After we hung up, Jeff had his own time with God, questioning and expressing his frustration and anger. He fought the feelings of being a victim, the lies from the enemy that he didn't matter, that God didn't truly love him. The unfairness of the situation washed over him. It was hard not to give in to self-pity when it seemed he had every right.

Jeff and I both arrived at a decision that night, confirmed over the course of the following days and weeks. It took time, and it was hard that we couldn't be together to hold each other during those times of intense grief. But, it sent us to the Lord, who is the real comforter and giver of peace that no person can bestow. We had our regular visits and talked and prayed, receiving strength from each other, but most of our time was working out our grief before God, each in our own way.

We both wondered, was this God's final answer? Was Jeff to remain locked up for the rest of his life?

We've never felt like God has answered yes or no to our earnest and persistent prayers for Jeff's freedom. But, we, and especially Jeff, have been waiting such a long time. We've often said if God would just tell us "no" we would stop fighting and settle into this life and accept it. But, the desire to pursue Jeff's freedom has not diminished, and we've never felt God saying it was time to give up.

So many questions, and no answers.

CHAPTER 27

WHAT'S NEXT?

To quote a children's book—Friday, January 7, 2011, was a, "Terrible, horrible, no good, very bad day."[6]

To say we were a bit shell-shocked would be putting it mildly. We went through all the classic emotions of grief: disbelief, anger, denial, numbness, acceptance. The feelings came to us in waves and not in any particular order.

For me, the hardest trial has been to not stay angry and bitter toward our now former governor. He went on to run for the office of Senator of the United States and won. I couldn't look at his ads on TV without feeling

---

6   Judith Viorst, Ray Cruz (illustrator), *Alexander and the Terrible Horrible, No Good, Very Bad Day*, (Atheneum Books for Young Readers; An imprint of Simon & Schuster's Publishing Division, Text Copyright, 1972, Illustration Copyright 1972)

a pit at the bottom of my stomach, bitter thoughts, or intense sadness.

To this day, I don't understand how someone could have all the information he had, the full board's recommendation, and, having the full authority to do so, then not decide to make things right. To be honest, at the time, I asked God not to give him a moment's peace until he set this right. But, to my knowledge, that didn't happen.

I knew, deep in my heart, I needed to forgive him. It has been more difficult than I would have imagined. I've been able to forgive a lot of things in my life, but this has been the hardest battle so far. I finally had to turn it over to God as I couldn't forgive on my own.

Jeff has had many of the same struggles, and we have often prayed together to find forgiveness in our hearts for Mr. Rounds.

If the governor had made the same decision soon after the board's recommendation in 2004, Jeff would have had the opportunity to repeat the process several times during his tenure. Maybe that's why the governor delayed his decision, knowing he could be facing the same dilemma year after year. We can only speculate.

As mentioned earlier, Jeff was deeply disappointed with the news. To wait this long only to be denied, seemed exceptionally cruel. The governor offered no reason for his decision. One of the attorneys called the board's office and heard there was an unusual note that came with the governor's denial to the board. It read something like, "Please make sure all of Jeff Howard's legal rights are preserved." We have not been allowed to see this note so can't confirm it.

My mind was filled with "What ifs?" But Jeff knew better than to get stuck in that thought pattern. He's had a lot more practice with letting go and purposefully looking forward with hope for the future.

We don't know what goes through Mr. Rounds' mind these days and if he ever thinks about Jeff. Maybe he hasn't had another thought, feeling he made the right decision. We just don't know. What we know is that what he thinks isn't important to us moving on. Our hearts have slowly mended, and we've learned to forgive.

CHAPTER 28

LOOKING BACK

Many things change in thirty-seven years. Earlier, I listed so many things Jeff has missed out on over the years.

I challenge you to think back to where you were thirty-seven years ago and look at how many things have happened in your own life. Who were you thirty-seven years ago compared to who you are now? What were you doing thirty-seven years ago compared to what you are doing now? How many changes have you had? What has changed for those you love? What losses have you experienced? Who has come and gone in your life? What celebrations have taken place?

It is staggering to realize what we might have missed if we were locked away and unable to be part of all that has happened in our world. What would our loved ones' lives look like without us? Who might not have even existed if we hadn't been there?

The realization of what he has missed, and continues to be left out of, is something Jeff faces, day after day, year after year. He enjoys being Grandpa Jeff to the grandchildren from my side of the family but wonders if he has grandchildren of his own and if he'll ever have the opportunity to meet them.

Pete went on with his life. Within the next couple of years, he would begin telling people that he had committed a murder and sent an innocent man to prison for it. We'll never know his motivation for confessing to his friends. Was he feeling remorse?

Why did Pete take his own life? Was he afraid someone would tell authorities, and he didn't want to go back to prison? Was he unable to live with what he had done?

We will never know the answers. We wish Pete had told the authorities or left a suicide note, so Jeff could be set free, but he didn't.

Pete's son was just a boy when he overheard his father tell what he'd done. According to his sister, it had an enormous impact on him and ate at him until the time he took his life as well. What if he had been listened to back then?

By the time of Jeff's habeas hearing in 1996, Pete and his son, Jason had both taken their lives. Three of the people who wrote affidavits concerning what Pete told them before his death, had also died.

In the motion hearing preceding the habeas hearing, where the state asked for a dismissal, the judge is quoted in response to the five issues raised in the habeas: "I guess there are five points in this motion. Judge Patterson is dead. He presided over the case and sentenced the petitioner... Everybody tells me—I guess I'll have to take their word for it—a key criminal trial witness, Pete, is dead and I guess that is important to the petitioner because Pete has recanted his testimony

to someone. I don't know who it was. Two other witnesses, and they are unnamed as far as I can tell, who
Howard states about his newly discovered evidence,
they are also dead.

"John Gridley, III, who represented Howard at the
trial, is no longer an attorney. His file is lost or destroyed.
And I guess Gridley also states that his memory is
fading.

"So I guess the question is should this habeas be
dismissed... I guess I'm going to deny it based on those
points that don't involve dead people...the state would
be prejudiced, I think, by having issues involving dead
people and people who can't testify."

What this meant is that the hearing could move
forward, leaving out any issues having to do with anyone
who was now deceased.

He went on to say that the defendant, Jeff Howard,
"Should have been a little more diligent since '89, but
he did file a new Petition in '94." The judge appears to
blame Jeff, who had been locked up with no resources
or people to advocate for him during that time.

It's understandable that the testimony would be
hearsay when people have died. But within a few short
years of Jeff's trial, six people had come forward with
Pete's admission of guilt. If action had been taken when
the information first surfaced, all six would have still
been alive.

Jeff was the one most prejudiced by these deaths,
as well as that of the presiding judge over his original
trial. Jeff was the most affected by his trial attorney's
lack of memory regarding the case and ability to recall
by reading case notes which the attorney destroyed.

Since the 1996 hearing and loss of further legal
remedies through the court system, others have also
passed away. The last of the four who came forward

stating Pete had admitted the killing, passed away soon after that hearing. Rick, who testified in 2004 at Jeff's commutation hearing, died in a motorcycle accident in September of 2011.

In February 2017, I visited Janice, Pete's ex-wife, who testified at the trial. We met at her daughter's home, and Stacey, Pete's daughter, was also at this meeting. Janice said she felt she was in a better place than when I met her in 1996 and wanted to do what she could to help. She had been surprised when told Jeff was still in prison. She had assumed Jeff was released after her brother, Scott, went to testify on Jeff's behalf in 1996.

Janice admitted she lied for Pete on the stand and that he hadn't come home the evening of March 5th. She didn't know where he was as he didn't involve her in what he did outside their home.

After the murder, Pete told her they needed to get married because of a case he was involved in, but she didn't know which one. Janice said you didn't question Pete—you just did what he told you to do. She didn't know much about his activities although she knew he had a case pending somewhere, she thought in Iowa.

He told her to lie and say he was home with her and that Jeff had admitted to killing his roommate. He even told her to lie on the polygraph. She was surprised the attorney still asked her to testify in court because she knew she had failed the polygraph.

Janice told those of us present, it haunts her that Jeff is still in prison and she had a part in making that happen. She decided it was time to make a formal statement about the truth and what she knew. She put her words into a legal affidavit.

People have sometimes said to us, after hearing the story, if only there were a "smoking gun." We've had a lot of "if only" thoughts. If only Jeff hadn't left town.

If only Pete hadn't killed himself. If only he'd left a suicide note. If only the police had considered Pete's involvement suspiciously and looked at him as a suspect. If only Scott had stayed and testified. If only Janice hadn't lied for him. If only. The list can go on and on.

But, you can't go back and change how things happened in the past. Moving forward is the only option.

CHAPTER 29

THE HERE AND NOW

A few weeks after receiving news of the governor's denial of Jeff's commutation in 2010, I asked friends and family to come to a meeting at my house to put our heads together to see what we could do next. Also present were the "law students," now attorneys, with a few years of real-world experience under their belts.

I think we all knew Jeff's legal options through the courts were exhausted, but the attorneys wanted to spend a little more time researching to make sure that nothing was missed. After all their training in presenting legal matters to the courts, it made sense to find a solution in their area of expertise.

A few other ideas were passed around. Maybe trying to gain publicity would help. Maybe we could sell the idea to news media. We wondered if that would help or hurt Jeff's cause.

We explored connections to the new governor, of which there were some. We had researched the current members of the Board of Pardons and Paroles and knew it was a very different group of people than those we had appeared before years ago.

This new board's track record had shown less tendency to recommend a commutation for lifers. Several members were known for their hardline stance on crime and criminals. We wanted to find another way besides coming up before this group. Honestly, I think we were still raw from the pain of the recent rejection and were afraid.

It was decided that since the Board of Pardons and Paroles had already done their homework and recommended a commutation in 2004, and there's no definitive law that says once a commutation has been recommended that you have to start all over, that we would go directly to the new governor and hope he might use the recommendation from the original parole board. We had plenty of time under his tenure to go back to the board and start over if we had to. We decided we would even ask him to consider a pardon.

The attorneys now had heavy caseloads of their own and busy lives, but, they pledged their continued support and to help in any way they could. I set about putting together the framework for a case for clemency to present to him.

I was working a demanding job and it took time. This wasn't my area of expertise either and a lot of time had passed since I'd reviewed the case. We had a couple of contacts who knew the governor and offered to help get the information to him. But first, we had to decide how to make our case for such an unusual request. To our knowledge, this had never been done before.

We also heard that our present governor is a stickler for following proper procedures, based on those who had worked with him in the private sector in the past, and those who know him now. But, we still wanted to try to arrange a meeting with him and plead Jeff's case.

We felt our best chance was having the attorneys, who had been with us all these years, present Jeff's case to the Governor, and they agreed to help when we had the case ready. Along this part of the journey, we have been joined by an exceptional and passionate paralegal, Kara, who has had years of experience in working in defense work.

When we started on this leg of the journey, Cheri, Jan, Bryan, and Matt, along with Kara, were all working in the Public Defender's office or Public Advocate's office, gaining new insights and experience.

Since then, Cheri ventured into private practice for a while but has since returned to her passion at the Public Defender's Office. Jan has her own law practice. Bryan now practices law in Texas but remains supportive of the efforts to find justice for Jeff. Matt has his own law firm and serves as a part-time tribal judge. Kara works for the former head of our county's public defender's office, who is now in private practice. They are all still passionate defenders of justice in the work they do.

In November 2016, a "Case for Clemency" was presented to the Governor's office, and our fears were confirmed when we were told to go through proper channels. It feels like we're back to the beginning—right back to where we started in 2004 with the Board of Pardons and Paroles.

We often ask, and are asked, why do things take so long? There's no easy answer.

We are not people with means and the attorneys have done all their work pro bono. We are so very grateful.

They all have full and busy lives—families, law practices, life and death matters, illnesses, etc.

Each time we move forward, it requires reacquainting ourselves all over again with the intricacies of the case; researching and refreshing on the details, case law, etc.

The only legal option left at this time is to again make our case to the Board of Pardons and Paroles. It's a group made up of individuals with varying backgrounds, whose role is to determine if a person has accepted responsibility for their crime and is ready to re-enter society. They are not prepared to decide on the guilt or innocence of a man—that was decided on by a court of law and a jury of Jeff's peers. We believe we have a compelling case that Jeff's conviction was the wrong decision, but it takes extra time and consideration for the board to grant a hearing of these circumstances. And then, it still requires a majority decision between the nine board members.

At the time of this writing—we are in the process of making our application to the board. The attorneys are drafting a letter to go with the packet that would best describe why Jeff Howard deserves a lesser sentence. We may dare to even ask for a pardon, but it's unlikely they will consider it.

CHAPTER 30

WHO WE TRUST

As we wait—sometimes patiently and sometimes not-so-patiently, we continually go to God to ask Him to renew our hearts.

We desperately need to find a way not to allow this to destroy us. Even more, we must find a way to have peace in the midst of such a grave injustice.

We ask God to remove impatience, bitterness, judgment, and anger. All those emotions rise so quickly to the top but can destroy us and what we have. We ask Him to replace sadness with joy.

Recently, I asked Jeff how he's honestly doing with all the delays. He admitted sometimes it's hard and he has his days of discouragement. He makes a choice daily to continue to trust God and shared that it's become easier to do that over the years as his faith continues to grow.

The prison is not a very positive environment. It is full of negative people who want others to be negative with them. Jeff can't "go" to a quiet place to spend time with God. But, he starts each day in the very early morning hours, before others are awake and the incessant noise of prison life begins. He opens his Bible and begins with God's word, devotional books, and time in prayer.

One of Jeff's favorite Bible passages is Romans 12:1-2, "Therefore I urge you, brothers and sisters, in view of God's mercy, to offer your bodies as a living sacrifice, holy and pleasing to God—this is your true and proper worship. Do not conform to the patterns of this world, but be transformed by the renewing of your mind. Then you will be able to test and approve what God's will is—his good, pleasing, and perfect will." (NIV)

We've learned that while there are people we trust, they are not infallible. They don't move as fast as we would like and sometimes they don't make the decisions we want. They mess up. And we do too.

Jeff will be the first one to say that going to prison likely saved his life. Many people he hung around with during those years before prison have died due to the lifestyle they lived. Jeff lived that lifestyle too until he was forcibly taken off the streets.

Jeff's story—our story—is still developing, and we don't know how it will end. But, I can say this: we will always hope for Jeff's freedom. I don't see that ever changing. But maybe what we hope for the most is different.

I recently watched a documentary about a medical team and doctor who contracted Ebola during the epidemic in Liberia. Dr. Ken Brantly shared:

"People ask me, 'Was it your faith that saved you?' Is that what healed me?"

Dr. Brantly answered: "In a very real way, it was my faith, that was our attempt to follow Christ, that got me Ebola. And, that changes my perspective on faith. Faith is not something that makes you safe."[7]

In our circumstance, I would say that "faith" is not something that necessarily earns you freedom—at least not in a physical sense. Faith is about assurance of things hoped for (Heb. 11:1a). What we "hope for" may have changed along the way. We long to see loved ones come to know the love of God. We long for healing for others deeply affected by this crime. We long to know intimacy with Jesus in ways it appears we can only know by sharing in His suffering.

We long to take this pain and come out on the side of knowing how much we are loved by the One who made us. We long for that Love to overflow onto others—for the larger story unfolding in God' kingdom.

It takes knowing the Giver of grace and love to live this life with a peaceful heart. For us, it begins with our relationship with God—each of us spending time with God on our own. And it begins with us continuing—even after all these years—with praying and spending time in scripture together to learn God's truth about how He sees us and to know Him better.

I've often thought that giving up on our dream for Jeff's freedom would be less painful. The hurt each time he receives a denial takes its toll. But, profoundly, our faith does not take a beating. Instead, it seems to grow stronger.

God's love doesn't fix everything. But knowing and trusting how much He loves us helps us to see Him

---

7   "Facing Darkness" a Samaritan's Purse Film released in 2017 - http://facingdarknessmovie.com

as good. It helps us view circumstances and people as He sees them.

God invited me to enter Jeff's story, which had been unfolding for many years. But, we've learned that there's an even bigger story that we're part of and we've learned to trust Him even when we don't know how our story will end.

NOTE FROM JEFF

For my beloved wife, Judee:

Thank you for believing in me. You have shown me unconditional love. You have sacrificed so much (Romans 12:1-2). Thank you for sharing your life with me. I know without all the prayers and our faith, we could not do this. Judee, I love you! Thank you for your courage to tell our story. You love me for who I am. Thank you! I am truly blessed!

Your loving husband, Jeff

TESTIMONIES

The first time I saw and spoke with Jeff at the South Dakota State Penitentiary I realized this man is the real deal! A pillar for the Lord in a very dark place. As I got to know him more and he shared his life's story I was amazed! How can someone suffer such injustice, yet be so filled with Gods love, joy and peace? In spite of all he has been through he is a remarkable representation of the love of the Father and the perseverance of Jesus Christ!

I often ask how could this happen to Jeff? Why did this happen? A whole lifetime spent behind bars, in prison separated from his wife and family. This I know: many have come into a saving relationship with their Lord Jesus because of Jeff's witness! Jeff has protected many in this rough environment, he has helped set many free from demonic bondage through his prayer and counsel. A father figure, a man of integrity, a man they can trust, such a solid immovable pillar! He is so well respected by the men incarcerated.

As I write this I tear up knowing Jeff is innocent yet still in prison. For over 20 years I have watched this man of faith stay filled with confidence and joy that one day he will be released and set free from this unjust imprisonment. My continuous prayed is that you, Lord, give Jeff his freedom and restore all the years the locust have eaten!—*Pastor David Schwab, Outreach/Evangelistic Pastor Church at the Gate*

—w—

I had the privilege of working with Jeff Howard for three years while I was a supervisor with a ministry working and providing jobs in the South Dakota State Penitentiary. Jeff was one of approximately 50 inmates I supervised. Working in a prison causes one to always be on high alert, working hard to be in tune with every one of your senses. Always watching, always listening, never relaxing and keeping your guard up at all times. When you work in a prison, one lesson taught immediately, and often repeated, is that you never trust an inmate. You are told, "They can earn respect and gain privileges, but they are never to be trusted."

In a setting like this, the character of a man is quickly exposed, and the gap between real and phony is firmly established. Ironically, on more than one occasion, staff at the prison mentioned to me that, "If anything ever goes down, Jeff Howard is the ONE guy I trust." If fact, one former correctional officer told me, "If there is ever a riot and the inmates take over, the first thing I would do is lock myself in Jeff Howard's cell."

I always looked forward to seeing Jeff on my days inside the walls. His kind demeanor, genuine humility, and sincere attitude made Jeff a stand-up guy... not only in prison, but in life! I'm not sure how you can be a man of character, honor, and integrity, when life has been cruel and dealt you a hand of injustice, but Jeff Howard finds a way to stay positive, look for the good, serve the Lord in any way he can, and remain hopeful for the future.—*Torrey Babb, President & Founder at The Mission Ball*

—◊◊◊—

I joined the M-2 program at the prison in 1982. This is where an outside person is paired with a man in prison to provide friendship and support. These relationships can be short or long, depending on the circumstances. Jeff was my tenth M-2 person.

I met Jeff through another M-2 in the visit room when visiting another inmate. I thought it would be nice to get to know him and be his M-2 someday. I asked for Jeff personally after one of my M-2 relationships had ended and hearing that Jeff's M-2 had passed on. It would be a little while before we were paired because he had been moved, but finally we were matched up and have been friends ever since.

We hit it off right away and found we had a lot in common. I shared with him about my family, farming for forty years, and my years as Director of Equalization in Douglas County, and he shared about his family, history, and life in prison. We discussed our faith and often read Bible passages together. I think I learned more from Jeff than I could contribute to him. It was good for me to be his M-2.

I visited Jeff almost every Saturday for about ten years, until I had to give up my car last year. I am 95 years old and am full-time caregiver for my wife. Jeff and I write letters now since I can't visit. I pray for Jeff and Judee every night and hope he can get out someday and visit me.—*Edgar Goehring*

—⚹—

I met Jeff in the summer of 1982. We were both serving life sentences. We became friends. In 1983. I got into some trouble, went to the hole, and didn't see Jeff for more than six years.

During the years that I didn't see Jeff many things happened. I was transferred to another prison, where I continued to get into more trouble. After four years there, I had a spiritual experience after praying that God remove my drug addiction, which God did. After having this experience, I decided to follow Christ and became immersed in AA and Bible studies and church services.

About one and half years later, I met Jeff again. He had made changes in his life also. He was now clean and sober about three years in AA and following Christ. I was shocked to see that Jeff had changed, as I am sure he felt the same about me. We became the best of friends and were great support for each other as we walked the path we chose.

My sentence was commuted twice, and I was released in 1999. Since that time, Jeff and I have remained in contact through letter writing, phone calls, and last year I was allowed back inside the walls to visit.

Over the years I have seen Jeff continue to grow in integrity, grow in maturity, and in his commitment to helping others. His walk with Christ in sincere. God's grace runs deep to change hearts and minds when we allow God into our lives. Jeff has truly allowed God to be the Lord of his life.

Having been locked up with Jeff for many years my ability to observe him was unique. I got the opportunity to see who he really was and is today. He is a fine man today, redeemed by God's grace. There are a lot of men who deserve to be in prison and who never change. Jeff is not one of these men. In my opinion, if ever a man deserves another chance, Jeff would be that man.—*Reid Holiday*

—〰—

When I went to prison I was a lost soul. I was always looking for anything to get me outside of my own self. I knew I needed God, I just didn't know how to find Him. I was in such a dark place. I knew who God was but considered myself to be on bad terms with him. I know that is nothing He would have said—He would have only said "my son has lost his way." It took me awhile to realize that though.

My uncle had done time on "The Hill", so when I arrived, I reached out to people who had known him. That's when I met Jeff Howard. What I noticed about Jeff is that he seemed to have found true happiness. I wondered how he could be so happy with as much time he was doing. I knew he had found his happiness in God and I wanted what he already had.

Jeff helped me out a lot as I chose to go after the happiness and peace he has, and now I have that too; it comes from Jesus Christ—the one who paid the price for our sins. Going to prison saved my life.

I really miss Jeff, my brother in Christ, but I'm not going back just to talk to him or see him and I know that makes him happy for me. I'll see him again in our everlasting life. Jeff, thank you! You have helped me become the man I am today.—*Robert (RC) Davis*

—〰—

One of the greatest joys in life is to be witness to the meaningful changes that occur in someone else's life. While I have only known Jeff since 2014, I have seen changes in Jeff's life and have heard about a great many others that Jeff has experienced. Certainly not least among them is the realization that in Christ we do not need to define our self by our lowest moment nor do we need to keep living in that moment.

I am grateful that Jeff has been an example to me and many others of learning from the past so that we don't repeat it and moving forward into a preferred future. When the joy of the Lord is our strength, the potential for change is always present within us.—*Rev. Rick Van Ravenswaay, Pastor at Faith Church, former Pastor at Cornerstone Prison Ministry*

ACKNOWLEDGMENTS

I have never considered myself a writer. I've known writers and I love to read. When I was young, my parents subscribed to Reader's Digest Condensed Books and I'd make myself read all of the stories so I'd be a well-rounded reader. My grandma was a librarian and helped me collect and read all of the Nancy Drew and Hardy Boys books.

Writers seem magical and mysterious to me. They have stories in their heads and can put it down on paper in a way that draws you into another world.

About ten years ago, I felt a nudge to write Jeff's story. But, his story, our story, didn't seem magical or mysterious to me—it was just our life. Over the years I've told people Jeff's story and they would say, "That sounds like a movie!" So, after I left my last job as director of a non-profit, I began to entertain actually writing the story. I ran it by some people and was encouraged to go for it and see what God would do with it.

In telling Jeff's story, I especially want our children and grandchildren, a myriad of other family members, and those who knew Jeff growing up, to know Jeff as a real person and who he has become; not just the infamous troubled young man who went to prison so many years ago. Many of Jeff's memories are of before he went to prison—a phenomenon not uncommon to those who are incarcerated. The same is true for people on the outside when they remember Jeff. They remember him as a young boy, and an angry and unsettled young man. But, many don't know Jeff and who he is today.

There are some people I want to thank for their encouragement to tell Jeff's story and our story. Without their help and support, I'm not sure I would have had the courage to turn this into a reality. I don't know how to list each person in order of importance. Every single person's contribution is important, so please know that wherever you land on these pages, every one of you is "my favorite" inspiration.

I felt so alone in the quest for Jeff's freedom until that fateful day when I met Cheri Scharffenberg. We had no idea how our lives would intertwine over the years. Cheri, when you brought in your colleagues and friends and took on Jeff's case—you gave us both hope! You inspire me as you continue to fight for truth and justice. I do not know how you do it, but I'm so grateful you do. Not only for Jeff, but for others.

Jan Olson, Matt Olson, Kara Duncan, and Bryan H. Thank you all for joining with us in the quest. You are all amazing and I can't thank you enough for your contribution in this journey. Thank you all for believing in Jeff and staying with us! Jeff and I are moved by your continued support.

Thank you, Linda Outka, my mentor and friend, for your encouragement and gracious insights into my life and giving me courage to explore and to trust who God made me to be, even if I am still figuring that out.

Thank you Kary Oberbrunner and the Author Academy Elite team for the support and encouragement you give! It is daunting enough to put a story into print—there is no way to put a price tag on the value you put into your authors to help make our dreams a reality.

Teri Capshaw, you have added creative and practical value as my editor. You've helped to calm many of my fears about publishing a book. It is so amazing that we can connect on so many levels. God is incredible in ways we rarely can comprehend. I know he sent me to you.

Holly Carnes, your ability to capture people in their best light is a blessing to those of us who find ourselves on the other side of the lens. Thank you for your patience and creative input on that really fun day!

A quote by Cosette Gutierrez, guided me in finding my beta readers: "If your mentors only tell you that you are awesome, it's time to find other mentors." I needed truth-tellers and you each provided unique and invaluable insights, and with much grace. Tamara Reeves: aka my daughter-in-law #2, who thinks very differently than I do. I value that a lot! Tim Schaeffer: I admire your inquisitiveness and passion. Your wife was right about you! And, Karen Emmer, my youngest sister: A gifted writer—I hope to see your stories in print someday. I cannot thank you all enough!

To my friends and family who have encouraged me along this journey, thank you, from the bottom of my heart. I started to name you, but I knew I'd leave someone out, and I don't know how my heart would heal if I wounded those I love so dearly.

To my husband, who inspires me every day—I pray I love you well. You deserve it. To my children who accepted Jeff into our family—thank you. You each inspire me in the men you have become.

Most importantly—thank you Jesus. You gave more than I could ever give. You are my inspiration, my courage, my strength, my love. You are my Savior. I cannot imagine my life without you.

81504442R00100

Made in the USA
San Bernardino, CA
09 July 2018